Saving the Corporate Soul

& (Who Knows?) Maybe Your Own

Saving the Corporate Soul

& (Who Knows?) Maybe Your Own

**Eight Principles
for Creating and Preserving
Integrity and Profitability
*Without Selling Out***

David Batstone

JOSSEY-BASS
A Wiley Imprint
www.josseybass.com

Published by Jossey-Bass
A Wiley Imprint
989 Market Street, San Francisco, CA 94103-1741   www.josseybass.com

Jossey-Bass books and products are available through most bookstores.
To contact Jossey-Bass directly call our Customer Care Department within the U.S.
at 800-956-7739, outside the U.S. at 317-572-3986 or fax 317-572-4002.

Jossey-Bass also publishes its books in a variety of electronic formats. Some content
that appears in print may not be available in electronic books.

Library of Congress Cataloging-in-Publication Data
Batstone, David B., 1958–
    Saving the corporate soul— & (who knows?) maybe your own: eight principles
for creating and preserving integrity and profitability without selling out/
David Batstone.—1st ed.
        p. cm.
Includes bibliographical references and index.
    ISBN 0-7879-6480-8 (alk. paper)
    1. Leadership.   2. Social responsibility of business.   I. Title.
HD57.7 .B378 2003
658.4'08—dc21   2002154858

Printed in the United States of America
FIRST EDITION
HB Printing   10 9 8 7 6 5 4 3 2 1

Contents

Saving the Corporate Soul

& (Who Knows?) Maybe Your Own

Introduction

Values Make the Company

A COMPANY'S VALUES—WHAT IT STANDS FOR,
WHAT ITS PEOPLE BELIEVE IN—ARE CRUCIAL TO
ITS COMPETITIVE SUCCESS.
—Robert Haas, Chairman, Levi Strauss & Co.[1]

"Think about how much of our lives we spend at work," the executive of a New York publishing house said wistfully to me. "Then consider how ambivalent—and perhaps a bit ashamed—most of us feel about the corporations who employ us. I know that I want my life to count for something more."

He is not alone. Corporate workers from the mailroom to the highest executive office express dissatisfaction with their work. They feel crushed by widespread greed, selfishness, and quest for profit at any cost. Apart from their homes, people spend more time on the job than anywhere else. With that kind of personal stake, they want to be part of something that matters and contribute to a greater good.

Sadly, those aspirations often go unmet. Trust in our financial and commercial institutions is eroding. Every day, the newspaper fills us in on the latest corporation to fall into financial misconduct and public deception. Insider trading on public markets, cooking the books, outlandish executive pay and perks, fraudulent research that covers up the harmful effects of products on people and the environment: a steady stream of scandals deeply scars the business landscape. "Business as usual," an expression that once implied steady confidence in the flow of financial exchanges, now sounds the alarm to watch your back—if not your wallet.

Truth be told, the corporate crisis is as much spiritual as it is financial. Yes, fortunes are won or lost on the ability to anticipate trends and create products that meet those demands. But capitalizing on innovation is not enough today. A company's success also hinges on whether in the eyes of its employees and the public it honors a common sense of justice.

"Whatever company I work for in the future, I'll never again trust at face value what top executives say." A deep sense of betrayal marks these words spoken by a Global Crossing vice president who was laid off just weeks before the broadband telecommunications company filed for federal bankruptcy protection amid questions about its accounting. Along with thousands of other Global Crossing employees, she did not receive severance pay. "When top executives laid us off they must have known they were going to file bankruptcy and that they'd never have to pay us severance," she says, adding that some senior officials left the company with generous exit packages. "Maybe what they did was legal, but it feels unethical, especially when you look at how they treat themselves."[2]

Workers are six times more likely to stay in their jobs when they believe their company acts with integrity, according to Walker Information, a research company that measures employee satisfaction and loyalty at the workplace. But when workers mistrust their bosses' decisions and feel ashamed of their firm's behavior, four out of five workers feel trapped at work and say they are likely to leave their jobs soon.[3]

To thrive, corporations need to take account of this crucial shift in social values. Dispirited workers do not perform well; low morale saps the passion and creativity that otherwise would be unleashed on behalf of a company's mission. Corporate workers are looking for a new vision, a path to save the corporate soul. And just maybe their own.

Soul Searching

What is it about the corporation that makes joining it feel as if we're making a bargain with Mephisto for our soul?

Nearly fifty years ago, my father launched his professional career in the corporate world, joining General Electric in a management training program. He then made a horizontal move to Union Carbide and finally fled the corporate world altogether a few years later to start a family-owned retail business. My dad could not point to any specific conflict he had with the corporation, and, now in retirement, he wrestles with the what-ifs had he stayed and patiently climbed his way up the corporate ladder. At the time, however, my dad deplored the feeling that he was becoming just another number in an impersonal organization, a cog in the machine.

In his 1956 classic *The Organization Man*, William Whyte gave ample evidence that my father did not face his spiritual struggle alone. Whyte showed that the growth of large organizations, while leading to vast economic and political changes, was having an equally dramatic impact on the individuals who worked inside them. Their collision with the corporate structure stripped workers of a sense of uniqueness and forced them to make decisions not of their own choosing. These observations led Whyte to a radical conclusion: "We do need to know how to co-operate with The Organization but, more than ever, so do we need to know how to resist it."[4]

That legacy is still deeply rooted in our popular consciousness. Recall the number of movies you have seen that feature heroic characters who fight against the greed of a corporate giant to save their community. Hollywood has made an icon of the underdog fighting incredible odds to do the Right Thing.

Is it really meaningful, then, to talk of a corporate soul? After all, the corporation was created in part to protect individuals from being held personally responsible for the actions of a public entity. It also offers a more efficient structure for aggregating capital that yields the potential for higher profits. None of these objectives depends on promoting the dignity and worth of individuals or their communities. The corporation's harshest critics in fact depict it as a cold, calculating machine.

In this book, I will show that a corporation has the potential to act with soul when it puts its resources at the service of the people it employs and the public it serves. That journey begins once a company seeks to align its mission with the values of its workers. It is unrealistic to expect that all of the workers' values will match those of the company, of course. But when that alignment moves closer together, the morale of the company is transformed.

Precisely for that reason, senior managers need to step back occasionally from the tyranny of the urgent and ask their own people, "Why is it that you want to work here?" If workers cannot get inspired about the company, they will not communicate a compelling message to customers. A vital corporation helps its people to think, plan, and express their dignity in the way they carry out their daily tasks on behalf of the enterprise. In other words, it tends to its soul.

Workers, in turn, need to evaluate honestly what their company stands for. If its core ethos violates their personal values and they are unable to change the environment to align who they are with the real company mission (rather than the published one), then it may be time to start looking for a new place to work.

The market alone cannot guide our decisions. Although the market is a dynamic platform for producing meaningful social goods, it is inherently bent toward impersonal ends. Read Tom Higa's story, which follows, and I think you will agree.

How Much Is Enough?

Tom Higa operated his Chevron gas station on a corner block in San Francisco for over twenty-five years.[5] It was the old-fashioned kind of shop where the attendant would wash the windows and kick the tires. Tom began working at the gas station as an attendant in 1964. After eight years of hard work, he took over as owner and picked up the station lease with Chevron.

Tom is exceptionally popular in his community. He hired locally over the years and provided a high quality of service to his customers. In turn, Tom owes a great debt to his neighbors. They saved his business.

Back in 1989, Chevron gave Tom the shocking news that it would not renew his station lease. The underground storage tanks on the property were in need of replacement at a cost of about $150,000. Oil company officials told him that the station was outdated and no longer matched the image of what a Chevron station should look like.[6]

Tom didn't see it coming. He had consistently met or surpassed the gas sales Chevron had set for his station; in fact, his operation was returning a healthy 12 percent profit margin on average. "I wasn't going to become a millionaire, but I earned enough to keep my family secure and deliver a good return to the corporation. I don't know what profit level it would take to satisfy Chevron," wondered Tom.[7]

The financial analysts back at Chevron headquarters indeed had crunched the numbers and concluded they could do better. By closing Tom's business, demolishing the station, and building a commercial building on the site, the property could return at least a 15 percent profit margin. Chevron corporate saw it as a clear-cut business decision to maximize profits.

Tom went into a panic. What other livelihood could a man nearing fifty with two young children and a lifelong career at a gas station pursue? Chevron officials suggested he might enter a computer-training course. To Tom, the idea was absurd; such a career detour did not match his skill set or his interests. He knew what he had a passion for, and that was running a gas station.

The neighbors were upset as well. They wanted a service station in the community, not another commercial building. "The whole neighborhood loves this place," remarked one of Tom's long-time customers. "They're honest and friendly and trustworthy, and they give real good service. Isn't that the kind of image a company wants?"[8]

The neighbors leaped into action. They sent hundreds of letters and a long list of signatures on a petition to Chevron urging the corporation to reconsider. Copies also were sent to San Francisco's city hall, and they landed on the desk of Mayor Art Agnos.

Agnos backed a thriving private sector in his city, but he also took seriously his responsibility to protect the interests of citizens.[9] He placed a call to Chevron's corporate headquarters, and within days, one of its senior managers paid a visit to his office.

The mayor asked the Chevron manager whether the neighborhood had presented an accurate picture of Tom Higa's business. Did Tom really hit his numbers for gas sales quarter after quarter? Yes, the manager confirmed, but then went on to review the business case for Agnos, emphasizing how the corporation could raise its profit margin with the execution of its plan.

Agnos searched for a compromise. How about delaying the plan for another eight to ten years until Tom was closer to retirement age? No, the manager responded; the company was determined to move forward now.

His stubborn and callous attitude angered Agnos. The mayor informed him that Chevron's plans to develop the property might not go as smoothly as the company had projected. In fact, he threatened him on the spot with a stringent environmental impact procedure that in all likelihood would lead to delays and substantial unforeseen costs.

A pitched political struggle ensued in San Francisco. The details will not be fully recounted here, but suffice it to note that Agnos and the city council went ahead with the environmental impact legislation, Chevron's plans to repurpose the property were thwarted, and Tom Higa's Chevron went on to operate at a healthy profit for another decade.

There's an added behind-the-scenes piece to this drama that underscores the values at stake. While he was mayor, Agnos held a quarterly luncheon with the chief executive officers (CEOs) of the major corporations with headquarters in San Francisco. The atmosphere turned chilly shortly after the mayor's showdown with Chevron. Agnos recalls entering the dining room to an awkward silence. Moments after all were seated to begin lunch, the CEO of one of California's major banks raised his voice so that all gathered could hear: "Arthur, you realize that we're pretty upset at you over this environmental legislation."

Agnos paused a second before replying, "Okay, I guess that's understandable, but let me give you my perspective. Here's a man with a family to support, owner of his own franchise for sixteen years, and the business is thriving. Then a wealthy corporation announces it's going to shut him down. He's always made money for the company, yet some green analyst in headquarters figures on paper the company can make a few percentage points more. So let me ask you something: How much is enough?"

All conversation and movement came to a stop. Agnos, it seems, had uttered an unpardonable blasphemy. The bank executive came back with emotion: "Arthur, the very fact that you can ask that question terrifies me."

Agnos let another agonizing half-minute pass, each player waiting for the next move in this awkward chess game. He then drove home his point: "So, guys, I ask you again: How much is enough? Since no one has responded, I guess the answer is that there's never enough, no matter what the cost."

Agnos had raised the relevant question: How does a business calculate the cost of personal livelihood and community vitality? For the financial analysts at Chevron, at least, the Right Thing to do lies plainly in front of us in the numbers.

But raw numbers can tell many tales. In this instance, the effort to close Tom's business may have ended up being more costly than Chevron had anticipated. It could not quantify the financial impact of a tarnished company reputation once the saga was dragged through the media. Nor could it calculate the strategic impact on other Chevron franchises once word spread that reaching, and even surpassing, targets for gas sales would not protect them from foreclosure. Finally, it could not put a financial figure on the low morale of Chevron employees at corporate headquarters, who surely felt something less than pride in their company's efforts. In short, a strong business case can be made that Chevron's decision to close down Tom Higa's service station was costly indeed.

FINDING COMMON GROUND

The vast majority of corporate executives would say, at least in their more candid moments, that their firm's public responsibility begins and ends with their shareholders. "What is enough?" you ask. "More than last quarter" is what they answer. That is the measure by which they are hired, compensated, and fired. It is also the plumb line that the stock market uses to reward or punish their companies.

Over the past two decades, public markets have tended to be unrealistic about the growth curve of individual enterprises. Even the best-run companies are subject to the rise and fall of economic cycles, but one bad quarterly earnings report these days and a company's stock gets hammered on the trading floor. This quarterly vision practically forces senior managers to look for short-cuts that will inflate short-term results at the expense of long-term sustainability.

For that reason, the burden for reinventing corporate behavior extends beyond the executive office. It is vital for other stakeholders who participate in the business web to reevaluate the ways they work, invest, partner, supply, and consume.

The problems at Enron, for instance, cannot be isolated to a small group of executives who looked to enrich themselves. When the going was good and Enron was reporting mind-blowing profits, few people cared that they could not make heads or tails of the company's financial statements. The desire to believe the illusion led lots of eyes to gloss over the obvious signs of chicanery. Once Enron started to stumble and report losses, the emperor's clothes fell off with startling quickness.

Given this landscape, I try to be very practical about what it takes to change corporate behavior. We are in dire need of senior managers who have the vision and courage to make good choices when the payoff may not be immediately apparent on the balance sheet. But in most cases, they will need to be convinced that doing the Right Thing will have a positive effect on their firms' bottom line, or at least will not add to the cost of doing business.

I realize that "doing the Right Thing" may seem quite subjective as a standard for corporate behavior. Business leaders rarely talk about the values that shape the character of a corporation and make an impact on its financial performance. But they do exist. In this book, I feature the following eight principles that I consider the most crucial for corporate performance:

Principle One: The directors and executives of a company will align their personal interests with the fate of stakeholders and act in a responsible way to ensure the viability of the enterprise.

Principle Two: A company's business operations will be transparent to shareholders, employees, and the public, and its executives will stand by the integrity of their decisions.

Principle Three: A company will think of itself as part of a community as well as a market.

Principle Four: A company will represent its products honestly to customers and honor their dignity up to and beyond a transaction.

Principle Five: The worker will be treated as a valuable team member, not just a hired hand.

Principle Six: The environment will be treated as a silent stakeholder, a party to which the company is wholly accountable.

Principle Seven: A company will strive for balance, diversity, and equality in its relationships with workers, customers, and suppliers.

Principle Eight: A company will pursue international trade and production based on respect for the rights of workers and citizens of trade partner nations.

Companies that incorporate these eight principles into their operations do not put themselves at a competitive disadvantage. In fact, substantial evidence indicates that principled companies excel financially over the long haul. Towers Perrin, the management consulting firm, took a close look at twenty-five companies that enjoy a strong reputation for public integrity and are rated year in and year out as desirable places to work. That model group includes well-known corporations like Southwest

Airlines, Johnson & Johnson, Applied Materials, and Procter & Gamble. Towers Perrin analyzed the market performance of these principled companies over a fifteen-year period and then compared their returns to those generated by public companies at large. The results: the principled companies delivered a total shareholder return of 43 percent, while the shareholder return of Standard & Poor's 500 performed at less than half that figure: 19 percent.[10]

A snapshot of Johnson & Johnson may offer a clue to why principled companies excel. In its corporate credo, Johnson & Johnson lists the stakeholders that its employees are asked to honor with their business decisions: first, customers; second, coworkers; third, management; fourth, the communities where the company operates; and fifth, shareholders. Lest we think that Johnson & Johnson is a philanthropic endeavor, the company credo also declares the obvious: "Business must make a sound profit." But the company does pledge that profit will not eclipse its other priorities.

In 1982, the Johnson & Johnson credo was put to the test when a major disaster hit. Eight people died from ingesting cyanide-laced Tylenol capsules. Johnson & Johnson executives made a decision immediately to recall 31 million bottles of Tylenol from store shelves even before the cause for the crisis could be determined. The company also promptly redesigned product containers and introduced tamper-proof packaging. Although Johnson & Johnson turned out to be blameless, the crisis ended up costing the company $240 million and cut its profits on $5 billion in revenues that year almost in half. But its decisive action ended up saving the Tylenol brand and generating a wave of goodwill from its customers.[11]

The Johnson & Johnson experience underscores why corporations would be foolish to sacrifice their credibility at the altar of earnings reports. Long-term market value does not rise or fall independent of a company's social impact. And like it or not, every action a corporation takes may be interpreted as a statement about what it stands for.

Accounting for the Good

If we had to settle on one philosophy that rules business operations today, it could be captured by this mantra: If you can't measure it, you can't account for it. That's precisely the reason that efforts to translate principles into corporate practices so often languish at the point of execution. Most senior managers today do feel an escalating pressure to conform to higher standards of integrity. But if they cannot understand how to identify and measure their outcomes, they are likely to consider principles a matter of image, not substance.

I hope to make it clear that a company's capacity to integrate the eight principles detailed in this book will enhance or (alternatively) diminish its overall business performance. The Towers Perrin study cited above indicates the potential impact on shareholder return over an extended period. There are three other prime areas where principles and their business outcomes can be assessed:

- A principled company will fortify its reputation.

- A principled company will be more likely to avoid costly lawsuits.

- A principled company will manage its business network more effectively.

Let's turn our attention first to reputation. Although it may seem the most intangible area of the three, it is a crown jewel among a company's assets.

Reputation: The Guardian of Your Brand

A brand is the visual, emotional, and cultural image that we associate with a company or a product. While the daily grind of business is about sales, brand building looks to create a bond and loyalty that lasts. Over time, customers develop a personal affinity with a brand; once they feel betrayed, their fury lashes out as it would toward a fallen politician or a movie star.

Reputation is not the same thing as a brand. We attribute character to people, and we do the same thing to companies. Reputation is the perceived character a company holds in the public eye. A company's reputation in large part depends on its ability to meet the expectations of a broad range of stakeholders.

A lot of companies have a strong brand but lack a well-established reputation. Sony and Pepsi-Cola, for instance, can boast solid brands, but neither company really has much of a reputation. When we think of Volvo, on the other hand, we think safety,

---

The Public's View

The public's impression of a company is most influenced by . . .

Contributions to social good: 56 percent

Brand quality: 40 percent

Business fundamentals: 34 percent

Source: *Corporate Social Responsibility Monitor 2001* (Toronto: Environics International, 2001).

which is a reputation holding up a brand.

Reputation serves as the guardian of the company brand. A company can take years to build a brand yet destroy it overnight with a soiled reputation. Arthur Andersen is a prime example of a firm that took a shortcut marked by dollar signs and undercut a brand that had been carefully cultivated over nine decades.

What People Look for When Choosing an Employer

Factor	Rating
Career growth potential	1
Strong corporate reputation	2
Starting salary	3
Fringe benefits	4
Record of high yield for shareholders	5
Good sports and social facilities	6

Source: Cone/Roper, *Cause-Related Trends Report: Evolution of Cause Branding* (Boston: Cone, 1999).

In today's business climate, reputation has become as important as brand. For starters, it is a key asset for attracting employees. A Cone/Roper study finds that corporate reputation is the second most important factor for people choosing an employer. Remarkably, job candidates rate reputation more highly than starting salary or fringe benefits.[12] People put a high premium on working for a firm that can be trusted.

Customers and investors also are highly influenced by a firm's reputation. Nearly four out of five Americans say they at least consider reputation when buying a company's product, and 36 percent call it an "important" factor in their purchasing decision, according to a survey conducted by Hill and Knowlton. The same study shows that more than 70 percent of investors consider reputation in their decisions even if that choice means lowering their financial returns.[13]

Now here's the bad news: consumers give very few companies high marks for reputation. Less than 2 percent of Americans surveyed look at U.S. companies as "excellent corporate citizens," and more than half rate corporations as "below average" in social responsibility.[14]

Going After Carrots and Avoiding Sticks

While some business leaders like to pin the spate of corporate scandals on a few rotten apples in the barrel, the American public believes they reflect more fundamental problems with the way corporations do business. In a Washington Post/ABC News poll, roughly three of four people viewed the malfeasance of WorldCom, Enron, and Global Crossing as "a sign of broader problems with the way many companies report their financial condition." Fewer than one in four believe that these scandals are "pretty much isolated incidents."[15]

The public thirsts for justice in the business world. If corporations are unwilling to take the steps necessary to amend their behavior, citizens will turn to the courts and legislators to set the standards. Historically, the levels of public trust in American business determine how much citizens look to their government to regulate business.

To date, the punitive stick has focused on a practice that the corporate world euphemistically calls aggressive accounting, and in many cases is nothing more than cooking the books. In April 2002, the Securities and Exchange Commission (SEC) levied a fine of $10 million on the Xerox Corporation, at the time the largest penalty ever given a public company in connection with financial reporting violations. As part of the settlement with the SEC, Xerox was forced to restate its earnings for a five-year period.[16] In levying such a stiff penalty, the SEC was sending a clear message to corporate America: if we can go after an established, well-respected player like Xerox, any company can be exposed and punished.

A business professor at the University of Pittsburgh, Jeff Frooman, measured the stock market's reaction to incidences of corporate misconduct. He took a close look at twenty-seven separate incidents when a corporation was slapped with punitive measures, such as regulatory fines, environmental lawsuits, and product recalls. The pattern he found should be a strong caveat to all who are responsible for corporate governance: offending companies suffered significant losses in shareholder wealth that in most cases they never recovered.[17]

Delivering on Trust Across the Network

The modern corporation does not live as an island unto itself. It swims within a sea of network-based enterprises that extend from manufacturing to distribution to marketing. As a result, many of a company's key relationship assets—the people whom it must trust to succeed—are located outside the corporate structure. Despite that fact, a firm is held accountable for every action that takes place in its name across the network enterprise. That fact alone should raise real concerns about the effectiveness of conventional structures of governance.

The operation of a business has a new level of transparency today. Because network-based enterprises are so heavily information driven, just about every policy, administrative action, investment, or transaction eventually reaches the public domain. Over the Internet, hundreds of millions of people have at their fingertips an effective tool for getting access to and sharing information. The higher the profile of a brand, the greater is the scrutiny of its activities.

Executives at Boise, the giant timber company, can attest to the daunting challenge this level of transparency creates. Over the past decade, Boise has faced intense pressure from consumers and distributors to end the harvesting of old-growth trees. At the prompting of environmentalists, a diverse group of customers including Kinko's, L. L. Bean, Patagonia, and the University of Notre Dame started boycotting the company's paper products. Explaining his company's decision to cancel its contract with Boise, John Sterling of the clothing company Patagonia, said, "There will always be companies that don't care where their lumber and paper come from, but as their customers become more sophisticated about environmental issues, they're going to have to pay closer attention to the practices of suppliers that sell them wood products."[18]

The consumer boycott and erosion to its brand forced Boise to reevaluate all its supplier relationships, and in March 2002, it announced that it would drastically reduce old-growth logging. An official for the timber industry, disappointed that Boise caved in to public pressure, complained, "It's blackmail any way you slice it. As more and more retailers fall victim to this extortion campaign, it could definitely have an impact on the industry."[19]

What this timber industry official fails to understand is that we have entered a new era. Network enterprises cannot ignore the values of their customers and partners. The savvy corporation will not treat public scrutiny as blackmail, but instead will see it as an opportunity to strengthen its reputation with customers.

Because environmentalists are holding the business enterprise accountable for its impact on the earth, most large corporations are putting protocols and standards in place to address their concerns. This book offers a blueprint to take action as well on other areas of public trust that are rising to prominence. Absent standards of accountability, a firm risks a reputation breakdown anywhere in its network.

Corporate workers often have to make decisions that will affect the lives of their fellow employees, customers, and the broader community. Yet most feel as if they are navigating through these prickly dilemmas without a compass. For them, my book will be a welcome guide. In each chapter, I feature real-life predicaments that confront the business enterprise and demonstrate how a principled company can meet the challenge. As useful as it is to identify the failings of business, it's more inspiring to show how companies can do it right. Hence, the lion's share of each of the following chapters will hold up best practices among corporations that are doing well by doing good. Along the way, I offer "vital signs" and practical tools that will help to monitor the application of my principle within any enterprise size.

Change can begin anywhere in the corporation. This book backs up that claim with solid evidence; a good number of the corporate innovators I feature do not hold an executive title. To make a major impact on the organization, however, an initiative eventually will need to gain the enthusiastic backing of leaders at the executive and board levels. They have the means to introduce new practices across the company and the responsibility to govern their execution. The importance of leading and governing with integrity is therefore where we will begin.

Chapter One

Leadership and Governance

Principle One

The directors and executives of a company will align their personal interests with the fate of stakeholders and act in a responsible way to ensure the viability of the enterprise.

Vital Signs

Has the company built a sustainable growth model geared for present and future earnings? Does the company make acquisitions that cohere to its business model? Do company directors fully disclose the compensation paid out to senior executives? Are directors and executives required to hold on to their shares and options while they are in the company's service? Are stock options reported as an expense on profit-and-loss statements? Are senior executives required to return stock options and performance bonuses if the company's earnings statements are revised downward due to fraud or mismanagement? Do directors grant sweetheart loans to senior executives? Is the wage gap separating executives from nonsupervisory workers excessive? Are the majority of the board members truly independent? Do company directors adhere to term limits? Are the voting majorities required to adopt shareholder resolutions attainable?

Directors who fail to direct and executives who fail to lead are at the root of what ails the corporate world today. A 2002 Watson Wyatt survey of nearly thirteen thousand American workers in all major industries found that fewer than two out of five employees trust their senior leaders. Only 63 percent of those surveyed can say their companies conduct business with integrity. "Unless [the corporation] can resolve the crisis of confidence among its employees, it has little hope of restoring the trust and confidence of investors that is so crucial in these economic times," declares Ilene Gochman, author of the Watson Wyatt study.[1]

We sorely need business leaders who bring integrity and passion to the way they go about their business. No one fits that bill more ably than Gary Erickson, the owner and CEO of Clif Bar, a leading maker of nutrition and energy bars based in Berkeley, California. The pressures endemic to a billion-dollar corporation are not played out fully at a small, private company like Clif Bar. But a reminder of what business can be—and how a true leader shares the risks and rewards of an enterprise—puts a spotlight on those practices at the top of the corporate ladder that cry out for change.

Raising the Bar

In 1990, Gary Erickson set off on a one-day, 175-mile bicycle ride.[2] At the time, he was a competitive cyclist and owned a wholesale gourmet bakery in the San Francisco Bay Area. As was his habit, he took along a six-pack of nutrition bars to keep up his energy levels. But nearing the end of the ride, he hit a wall. The distance did not grind him down; it was the final energy bar. "I just couldn't put the sixth one in my mouth," he recalls. "Why did healthy have to taste so awful?"

Gary returned to his bakery from what he now calls his "epiphany ride" with a revelation: create a tasty energy bar using all-natural ingredients. Clif Bar was born, named after his father, Clifford, with whom Gary had spent summers hiking in the Sierra Mountain range.

Gary and his business partner distributed their new product in bike shops exclusively at first and then sent samples out to thousands of natural food stores. They hit pay dirt. Orders started flooding in, and the company has been on a roll ever since. Launched in 1992, Clif Bar today is a top-selling energy bar in the U.S. market.

Shooting for the Luna

Let's probe a bit into Gary's business philosophy:

Dilemma: Why do most companies with successful products fail?

Hint: The same ill-conceived ambition tempts them to cut corners and violate responsible business practices.

Lesson: They become obsessed with growth and live beyond their means.

That may sound like strange wisdom coming from the CEO of a company that four years running made the list of *INC* magazine's 500 Fastest Growing Companies. Yet Gary preaches the gospel of sustainability: "Clif Bar shot up in the market, true, but we pursued a methodical, sustainable growth model."

Gary associates his business philosophy with his advocacy of sustainable agriculture. Nonsustainable farming methods, such as the heavy application of pesticides and fertilizers, can force a high yield out of the land. But the get-what-you-can-now mentality eventually meets its limit. In due course, the soil gets squeezed of all its vibrancy, and a law of diminishing returns kicks in. A business model that tries to squeeze growth artificially out of the market is equally ill fated, Gary contends.

Here's a classic nonsustainable business plan: the company sets growth targets based on what the shareholders determine its annual returns should be. To generate sufficient customer demand to justify those projections, the company implements a capital-intensive marketing campaign. More times than not, customer demand does not match expectations. Once the yield is lower than the capital planted, the company has to scurry to cover the shortfall. If the company does not have cash reserves on hand, it will have to go out and raise more (expensive) capital or find some other quick-fix solution.

Now note the difference in Clif Bar's approach. The management team sets its sales targets based on demonstrable product demand, above all taking into account the existing pipeline of product orders. With those figures at the top of their minds, they construct a financial model for the coming year that maximizes the company's potential for expanding its customer base while minimizing its risks. The management is careful not to overinvest in marketing: Clif Bar's marketing budget as a percentage of total expenditures is exceptionally low for the food retail market. That way, if the company has an off-year for sales, the damage is sustainable and the recovery is more natural.

Instead of relying on mass marketing, Clif Bar focuses on niches where customer surveys point to untapped opportunities. Its own research uncovered, for example, that women sports enthusiasts desired an energy bar geared to their lifestyle. But the Clif Bar line was too high in calories and lacking in minerals essential for women, such as calcium, iron, and folic acid. So in 1999, the company launched its Luna Bar line as a distinct brand for women. As part of its promotion campaign, the company sponsors a professional women's mountain biking team, Luna Chix, and boldly displays the Breast Cancer Fund label on all its wrappers. Within three years, Luna Bars were outselling the original Clif Bar line. It is highly unusual in any industry for a second brand to spin off and beat a highly successful first brand, and it is unprecedented in the nutrition bar industry.

Clif Bar's Recipe for Sustainable Growth

- Borrow capital only when absolutely necessary.
- Create strong customer demand.
- Find the right distribution partners.
- Base sales projections on the existing pipeline of product orders.
- Limit capital expenditures on marketing.
- Constantly test the market for untapped opportunities.
- Develop products to exploit new niches.

Staying on Stage

Gary once shared the ownership of Clif Bar with a partner, but they never could agree on the potential of a private company on its own to reach a national market. She feared that unless it grew rapidly, competition would kill the company. Her anxieties were heightened when food giants Nestle and Kraft acquired the company's two main rivals, PowerBar and Balance Bar, respectively. She lobbied to bring in outside money, particularly from a large corporation that could beef up Clif Bar's market muscle.

But Gary was reluctant to bring in new capital. He knew too many CEOs who had made the leap to build their business on outside money and subsequently turned into professional fundraisers. In his mind, it made them forget why they got into the business in the first place. "If the CEO is spending 50 percent of his time looking for money, what the hell is he doing with his vision?" he wonders.

The two owners came to a fork in the road when a major food behemoth offered to buy Clif Bar at three times its earnings. Gary would have walked away from the sale with an insane amount of money. After many sleepless nights wrestling over what he should do, he rejected the offer. He bought out his partner's stake immediately and became the company's sole owner.

Was his refusal to sell a standard case of a founder who cannot let go? Sort of, if that implies he did not want to give up on the dream that drove him to create Clif Bar in the first place. But more to the point, Gary realized that he did not want to exit the platform he had built. He liked the actors and script way too much.

Gary follows the European ideal of blending business and life. At Clif Bar, that starts by treating workers as partners. Cash bonuses are distributed to all employees annually based on a percentage of net profit without a cap; the more profit the company makes, the larger the bonus is. Worker well-being is another signature value at Clif Bar. Employees are paid for two and a half hours of physical exercise each week. Trainer-led workouts are offered daily; alternatively, employees can go at their own pace at the fitness club equipped at the office.

Gary also uses his business platform to push social causes he believes in. His mother is a breast cancer survivor, which explains in part his enthusiasm for Luna Bar's partnership with the Breast Cancer Fund. He in fact testified before a 2002 California State Senate hearing on breast cancer and the environment. On the ecological front, he established an in-house program to stimulate thinking on how the company can "work toward reducing our ecological footprint on the planet." Clif Bar has set a course to make its products 70 percent organic and is progressively converting its ingredients toward that goal.

Gary already has his dream job, combining his love for cycling, business, good food, and ecological activism. "I don't regret for a moment my decision to turn down our acquisition," Gary claims. "By keeping the company private, I can ensure the quality of our work environment, follow our own social agenda, and share the profits with those who come along for the ride."

WHERE DID ALL THE EARNINGS GO?

Somewhere along the road, corporations lost their way. Cashing in became their sole end, and nothing else mattered. They forgot about creating real value. Far too few enterprises are truly interested in laying the groundwork for a sustainable future. Senior managers seem more concerned about expanding corporate holdings than developing products, providing better service, or inspiring employees.

The Acquisition Binges

Even traditional blue-chip performers that over time have delivered strong earnings now rely on acquisitions to drive their growth rates. General Electric, for example, made over a hundred acquisitions each year from 1997 through 2001. This strategy for running a corporation led influential bond fund manager William Gross to complain that General Electric "grows earnings not so much by the brilliance of management or the diversity of their operations . . . but through the acquisition of companies."[3]

Executives of large public companies have turned into deal magicians, mesmerizing the stock market with a dazzling array of transactions. Once, Tyco chief executive Dennis Kozlowski was hailed as a hero on Wall Street. Over a three-year period, Tyco made over seven hundred acquisitions and created a conglomerate of companies with a disarray of products and distribution channels.

Whenever analysts pressed Kozlowski to explain Tyco's stunning market prowess, he offered only vague answers. In early 2002, evidence began to leak out that Tyco was manipulating its assets in a kind of sophisticated shell game, and its stock fell almost 80 percent, losing over $80 billion in value in a matter of months. Kozlowski and his chief financial officer, however, personally gained as much as half a billion dollars in profits by selling Tyco stock.[4]

It is easy to hide from investors how these acquisition binges put the company in a precarious position. Because the cost of capital can be quite low for large companies, the earnings of a new acquisition can easily outstrip the interest it pays on borrowed money. Initially, the results look promising on the balance sheet. But the company actually could be skating on thin ice. If interest rates rise or the company for whatever reason loses access to the short-term securities market, the firm's profits will take a nosedive.

Let's Make a Deal (Any Deal Will Do)

In my Introduction, I stressed that corporate greed does not emanate solely from the executive suite. David Sokol's story highlights how tough it can be for an executive to stay principled when pressure is applied to pump up the firm's stock price. In many respects, Sokol is the yin to Dennis Kozlowski's yang.

For most of the 1990s, David was the CEO of CalEnergy, an Omaha-based energy company.[5] A serious managerial challenge surfaced in January 1998 when, in the throes of the Asian financial crisis, the government of Indonesia renounced a major contract with CalEnergy. Half a dozen U.S. competitors, Enron among them, also suffered project cancellations.

David received the bad news from Jakarta on Friday. "Neither the analysts nor investors wanted to hear the bad news," he recalls. "They urged us to find a way to hide the event or cover it up with positive announcements about new deals."

Rejecting their counsel, David announced first thing Monday morning an $87 million write-off on two large geothermal projects, both nearing completion. He anticipated the fallout from Wall Street would be muted since the casualties would hit evenly across the energy industry. But to his shock, not one of his competitors revised their numbers. Wall Street hammered CalEnergy's stock while the share prices of his competitors held up reasonably well.

One year later, David reached the end of his patience with the public market. Several analysts advised CalEnergy's management that it needed to announce more deals; otherwise, the company would not be viewed positively on Wall Street. David replied that the company was doing all of the business that it could handle. Their reply: "You don't have to make good deals. What you need is deal velocity."

Fed up with the game, David put his own money up front and recruited a small group of investors to take the company private in 1999. CalEnergy's president joined him as did Warren Buffett, in Berkshire Hathaway's first foray into the utilities sector. By the end of the year, CalEnergy had become MidAmerican Energy, and its revenues had soared to $4.1 billion.

David Sokol exemplifies many of the same traits that make Gary Erickson of Clif Bar such a compelling leader: a dogged determination to build real value at the core of their enterprise and the courage to act with integrity as they go about their business. These qualities are essential if a connection is going to exist between a leader and the people who make the company work.

REMODELING THE EXECUTIVE OFFICE

Shareholders today are troubled not only with the executive who commits a criminal act, but also the one who puts personal gain ahead of the company's welfare. Perhaps the most galling part of recent corporate scandals is the contrast between the fortunes made by executives and the ultimate fate of their companies.

Unfortunately, it will take more than a few heroic CEOs to address the leadership crisis that confronts the corporate world. It calls for major reform in how executives do their job, how they are compensated, and how they are kept accountable. To do anything less underestimates the breakdown that led to widespread financial manipulation and greed. Here's my blueprint for remodeling the executive office.

Step One: Restore Sanity to the Compensation Structure

In 1980, the average CEO of a large firm made forty-two times as much as nonsupervisory workers. At the time, Peter Drucker warned that such a large pay gap might compromise the integrity of corporate leadership because it makes a mockery of the role of all the other workers in making the company hum.[6] Evidently, no one at the top of the corporate ladder was listening. By 1995, the ratio of inequality between the shop floor and the executive suite had increased to a multiple of 160. Then, over the next five years, CEO compensation went through the roof; in 2000, CEOs were paid 458 times as much as ordinary workers.[7]

What is worse than mockery? Disdain. That's exactly how many rank-and-file workers feel they are being treated. Defenders of generous executive pay packages like to point out that other highly talented individuals, such as sports superstars and entertainers, rake in otherworldly compensation as well, but at least athletes and actors are paid on the basis of their performance.

A *Financial Times* study found that senior executives and directors in the top twenty-five companies to go bankrupt from January 2000 to June 2001 amassed a collective fortune of $3.3 billion, even as hundreds of billions of shareholder value and well over 100,000 jobs were lost.[8]

Christos Cotsakos exemplifies the problem. The chief executive of the E*Trade Group made more than $80 million in cash and stock in 2001 even though his on-line brokerage firm reported a $240 million net loss. With E*Trade's profits down and its stock far below its high, investors rebelled. To settle a shareholder lawsuit, Cotsakos forfeited $21 million of his pay in 2002; when criticism continued to mount, he gave up an additional $16 million to E*Trade's employees.[9]

Leaders who have the ability to run a major corporation deserve to be compensated well. But talented executives are not that rare. Instead of going off on a costly search for superstars, corporate boards should be looking much more proactively for emerging in-house leaders who have proven themselves. Homegrown leaders tend to be better trusted within the company and will not command a king's ransom.

Corporate boards also would do well to heed the rumblings of rank-and-file workers like Robert Hemsley, who operates industrial machinery at a paper mill in Everett, Washington. The CEO of Robert's company receives 592 times more pay than he does. That fact did not make it any easier for Robert and his coworkers to accept management's warning of job layoffs in 2001 if mill workers were unwilling to take a pay cut. To rub salt in the wound, Robert's CEO received a stock bonus worth $1.4 million after workers made the demanded concessions. "I do not want to belong to a country club or own a suit," says Robert, clarifying that it is not pay envy that overwhelms him. "I just want to work at the mill until I retire."

In a moving op-ed published in the *New York Times*, Robert makes the case that avarice has replaced risk taking at the executive level: "I wonder if corporate executives appreciate the role workers play in their success. Free enterprise is a system of risks and rewards. As it now stands, employees suffer most of the risks, while executives enjoy most of the rewards."[10]

Step Two: Put Executives and Shareholders in the Same Boat

The demand to link executive compensation with company performance is not new. In the late 1980s, institutional investors already were complaining about exorbitant executive salaries, especially when their firm's profits were flat or declining. As a response, boards started giving out large piles of stock options to their senior managers.

A brief description of stock options may be helpful here. Options give the holder an opportunity to buy company stock at a set price, known as the strike or exercise price, over a stipulated period of time into the future (usually ten years). The strike price is commonly the market price on the date the options are granted. The grantee can either keep the stock or sell it on the open market, typically once the market price rises above the strike price. Theoretically, stock options should reward senior managers for stellar company performance.

It turns out that linking executive wealth to the company's stock price can have the opposite effect of what was intended. Managers have an incentive to pursue every possible path to improve the earnings they report, regardless of its impact on company health. "This . . . incentive method for top management is a grand social experiment that often turned managers into market manipulators, . . . boosting the market price at the expense of fundamental value, and even occasionally fudging earnings," warns Yale economics professor Robert Shiller.[11]

Boards now must retreat and restructure executive compensation policies. It would be a crucial first move to require top managers to hold a significant portion of their company shares—75 percent is the benchmark that I favor—for as long as they work at the company. A couple of important amendments could be tagged on to this policy: executives would be free to sell their company stock following a one-year cooling period from their departure, and if they choose to exercise any portion of their options during their tenure, they would be permitted to sell shares sufficient to cover their income taxes.

Under my proposal, executives would not profit from short-term blips in stock prices, including those caused by improper accounting or overly optimistic predictions. As former U.S. Treasury Secretary Paul O'Neil argues, "Stock options are not a short-term reward; they are a long-term incentive to do the right thing."[12] Larry Ellison, Oracle's chief executive, may not buy into that concept. During the first quarter of 2001, he took a much-publicized shot at Microsoft for lowering its earnings forecast. Ellison crowed that Microsoft's products, and not the economy, were to blame. One month later, Ellison made his first sale of company stock in nearly five years, for a personal gain of almost $900 million. Fast-forward yet another month, and there was Ellison back on stage, now announcing that Oracle would not meet its profit estimates. The stock dropped 21 percent in one day.[13]

Holding periods would reinforce the right priorities for top managers. They also would neutralize the privilege of insider information, ensuring that investors and managers face rough waters together in the same boat. Option packages would make executives abundantly wealthy when—and only if—their companies are successful over a sustained period.

A handful of corporations already practice this policy. At Bank One, for instance, the top fourteen executives must hold 75 percent of all stock the company gives them, whether they are outright stock grants or shares they buy when exercising options.[14] Sadly, more widespread application of this policy in U.S. corporations seems far off. At present, fewer than 10 of the 250 biggest American companies require executives to hold a large part of the shares they receive.[15]

Step Three: Expense Options—It's the Real Thing

Stock options can be worth hundreds of millions of dollars or more, but unlike executive salaries and bonuses, they do not show up as an expense on the balance sheet. Under current rules, a firm has to show only the number of options granted to executives, not their economic value. The real financial state of the firm then is somewhere hidden in the margins.

Standard & Poor's, the private bond-rating agency, announced in 2002 that it would reconcile corporate financials to account for one-time expenses, pension fund earnings, and stock options. Its redux of core earnings for the five hundred largest companies sliced reported profits by an average of 25 percent.[16]

Shouldn't every shareholder also know how his or her holdings are affected by options? Changes in the accounting rules would make those costs less opaque. When stock options are not treated as an expense, companies throw them around like free money. Options, however, do cost shareholders; their holdings are diluted by the issuance of any additional stock. If every option represented a direct hit to the bottom line, boards would be more discerning in their distribution.

Defenders of the status quo contend that a change in the rules would hurt nonexecutive workers, since companies would be sure to cut options to them first. That argument seems a bit specious when we consider that the top five executives of public companies hold 75 percent of all options distributed.[17]

The Coca-Cola Company helped to push the ball down the field when, breaking rank with the vast majority of American corporations, it boldly chose to voluntarily expense options in July 2002. The significance of the move was enhanced by the company's solution to the thorny problem of valuing stock options.

Opponents to reform have argued in the past that expensing options was meaningless because it was impossible to calculate the worth of options at the time that they ultimately would be exer-

---

Who Has Corporate Options?

Distribution of All Stock Options Outstanding as of 2000

Top five company executives	75 percent
Next fifty executives	15 percent
All other employees	10 percent

Percentage of Nonexecutive Employees with Stock Options, by Salary Range

$75,000 or more	12.9 percent
$50,000 to $74,999	4.2 percent
$35,000 to $49,999	1.5 percent
Less than $35,000	.7 percent

Source: D. Leonhardt, "Stock Options Said to Be Not as Widespread as Backers Say," *New York Times*, July 18, 2002.

cised. But Coca-Cola devised an ingeniously simple method. The company asked multiple investment banks to place bids on the options and arrived at an average as the operating valuation. This process gives companies and investors a fair reflection of the market value of options.[18]

The Achilles heel of this method is the conflict of interest inherent in a firm's relationship to investment banks. An investment bank might low-ball an option valuation, for instance, in order to win that company over as a client. The fact that investment banks in recent years have tried to buy influence with favorable analyst reports amplifies concern.

The hurdle is not insurmountable, however. An independent board could monitor the bidding process and catch patterns of suspicious activity by individual investment banks. Offenders would have to be punished severely enough to make the costs far outweigh the potential benefits of risking a violation.

Step Four: Stop the Pandering

"A gorgeous woman slinks up to a CEO at a party and through moist lips purrs, 'I'll do anything—anything—you want. Just tell me what you would like.' With no hesitation, he replies, 'Reprice my options.'"

Warren Buffett spun this jocular tale in his annual letter to Berkshire Hathaway investors in 2001 to illustrate how closely executive compensation resembles a seduction game.[19] In a fit of blatant pandering, boards have acted to shelter top management from falling stock prices. While some boards merely make performance goals easier to reach, others simply reprice the executives' options; nearly two hundred major companies swapped or repriced options paid out to top management in the first quarter of 2002 alone.[20]

Barring extraordinary circumstances, the practice of repricing options should cease. It sends out the wrong message to the entire company. It is hard to hold nonexecutive employees to standards of excellence when their leaders are being patted on the back for mediocrity.

Step Five: Draw the Line Against Misconduct

When Joseph Nacchio sat in the chief executive office at Qwest Communications, he frequently crowed about the company's consecutive streak of meeting analysts' quarterly estimates. What was the secret to his success? the rest of the business world wondered. Now we know.

From 1999 to 2001, Qwest appears to have swapped telecommunications capacity with other companies and then counted the phantom activity as revenue. During that period, Nacchio cashed in $227 million of company stock, and Philip Anschutz, a member of Qwest's board and largest shareholder, garnered almost $1.5 billion selling company shares. Qwest has been forced to readjust its numbers, but its admission of improper accounting will have no impact on the stock sales of executives and directors in positions of leadership at the time.[21]

Sound like fair play? Of course not. Top managers and directors should be required to disgorge stock options and performance bonuses if the company's earnings statements are revised downward due to fraud or mismanagement. They also should be forced to return the gains from sales of company stock made less than a year before bankruptcy.

Teddy Roosevelt hit the nail on the head almost a century ago: "We draw the line against misconduct, not against wealth. The capitalist who, alone or in conjunction with his fellows, performs some great industrial feat by which he wins money is a well doer, not a wrong doer, provided he works in the proper and legitimate lines."[22]

Step Six: No One Calls Me Sweetheart

K-Mart investors and workers were outraged in early 2002 to learn that loans were granted to their executives even as the company was on the verge of becoming the largest retail bankruptcy in U.S. history. Most controversial of all, the K-Mart board had forgiven $5 million it lent to its CEO, Chuck Conaway.[23]

K-Mart's imprudence seemed outrageous at the time. Then along came revelations that WorldCom had gifted its chief executive, Bernie Ebbers, a low-interest loan (2.3 percent) in the amount of $408.2 million and Adelphia had loaned $2.3 billion to John Rigas and his kin.[24] All of a sudden, the K-Mart loan deal seemed like a blue light special.

Executive loan programs were introduced in 1975 when Control Data Corp., a computer and financial services firm, offered them to stimulate stock purchases among company management. The company later agreed to forgive the loans (hence the term *sweetheart loans*) if managers met relatively stringent performance goals.[25]

The gifting of executive loans blossomed along with management stock option programs during the 1980s. A survey of large companies by Mercer Human Resource Consulting finds that almost one in four today offer some kind of loan to their top managers.[26] But the performance goals have disappeared; in practice, the forgiving of loans has become a popular way of disguising excessive compensation.

Outraged, Senator Charles Schumer of New York, who introduced a U.S. Senate bill to ban insider loans, asked the right question: "Why can't these corporate executives go to the bank like everybody else?"[27] Sweetheart loans just beg for conflict of interest and abuse. Boards need to be transparent about how they're paying top management. Then let them prove they are worth it.

DEALING WITH FAME

Most of my proposals for reform put the onus of responsibility on corporate boards. For years, the duty of board members could be satisfied by doing little more than standing up and waving when their names were called out at the annual meeting. More recently, due to pressure from investors and the growing incidence of shareholder lawsuits, directors are coming to terms with a new reality. They are being asked to take on a critical business function.

When the Enron scandal blew up, shareholders and employees appropriately vented their ire at the company's board of directors. Even the board had to point an accusing finger at itself: "After having authorized a conflict of interest creating as much risk as this one, the board had an obligation to give careful attention to the transactions that followed," the Enron board's special investigation committee concluded. "In short, no one was minding the store."[28]

Reading the Enron report for the first time jogged a memory of my own experience as a board member when I didn't feel as if our board had minded the store very well either. In the late 1990s, I joined the board of Fame Studios, an entertainment company based in Stockholm, Sweden. The chairman of the board at the time was Christer Sturmark, a very successful Swedish entrepreneur. Fame Studios was formed around the genius of a singular Web designer who asked Christer's help to build his small shop into a robust business. Christer brought in a bevy of world-famous musicians as investors, including Björn Ulvaeus of Abba and Per Gessle of Roxette. A management team was hired and a board of directors established, with Christer as nonexecutive chairman.

Just as the new CEO came on board, a past financial indiscretion came to the light. Back when he was running his one-man shop, the designer had failed to pay all of his corporate taxes on time. No worse sin could a Swedish company commit. The error was a matter of public record, accessible to any journalist who chose to carry out an in-depth investigation of the company.

Due to the celebrity profile of the company, even the smell of impropriety had the potential to turn into a media circus. Christer noted the risk and strongly advised the board to craft a press release immediately owning up to the past, with assurances that the new management had cleaned up the books. "It's one of the fundamental things I learned about running a company," Christer told the board. "If you have a crisis of any kind, face it head on and disclose everything completely. The worst thing we could do is cover it up."

Several of the other Swedish board directors leaned toward saying nothing. Putting dirty laundry out for public display did not seem to be the most effective public relations strategy. We had done nothing wrong, so why should we put out an announcement that implies mismanagement? The board did not vote down Christer's proposal, but the idea was shelved for later action.

It turned out to be a poor decision. Several months later, the leading financial newspaper in Stockholm ran a front-page story that was not at all kind to Fame Studios with this headline: "Company Owned by Pop Stars and Christer Sturmark Not Paying Its Taxes." By then, we regretted that we had not heeded Christer's counsel.

The best directors are chosen by virtue of their hard-earned wisdom and integrity. An influential network is valuable, yes, but it is even more vital to have guides who have traveled down the road already. They are likely to sense trouble brewing on the horizon long before it becomes a crisis.

Taking Charge of the Wheel

The character of the corporation takes shape first and foremost in the boardroom. Investors, employees, customers, and community groups are not privy to the confidential discussions that transpire behind closed boardroom doors. It is the board's duty therefore to ensure that the best interests of all stakeholders are honored.

That's the theory; in practice, CEOs are running the show. They orchestrate board meetings, hand-pick directors, and dole out bits of information. Sad to say, the directors usually put a rubber stamp on any proposal that comes out of the executive office. Corporate directors by and large are unwilling to challenge or even follow up on even the most routine matter.

A fortified system of checks and balances must be put in place at the heart of the corporation. My platform for reform features seven key proposals.

Proposal One: Boards Must Be Genuinely Independent

Even when the board has an outside nominating committee in place, the CEO typically wields control over the selection of board members. CEOs understandably want board members who are agreeable to their agenda, but to be effective, company directors should be free from compromising ties to management.

All kinds of bells and whistles should have gone off for Adelphia investors and employees when they saw that five of the nine directors were members of the Rigas family. Because they controlled the board and top executive positions, it was easy for the family to use the company as their own private piggy bank.

To minimize such occurrences, the New York Stock Exchange (NYSE) wants its publicly listed companies to make at least half of their board members independent. That step would represent progress; at the moment, roughly one-fourth of the companies on the NYSE still function with a minority of independent board members.[29] But these recommendations are still too tepid. There is no good reason for the chief executive to have more than one additional member (besides him or herself) representing management interests, for example. Top managers own collectively less than 5 percent of the company's stock in most cases. With more than one seat, they would be in fact overrepresented.

Advocates of the status quo argue that without adequate representation by top managers, the board would be isolated from actual business operations. To a degree, they have a legitimate point, which is why I do not favor a board completely free of management representation. But not voting as a director does not preclude senior managers from giving regular presentations to, and having regular discussions with, the board.

Board candidates ought to be expected to disclose any entanglements that compromise their independence, as should directors if their circumstances change. *Outside* does not mean the same thing as *independent*. A director's fee is the only compensation a board member should receive from the company; suppliers and paid consultants have their role, and it's not on the board. The NYSE stipulates that a board member does not qualify as independent if he or she is an employee, or even a former employee who has left the company within the previous five years. That's also a good benchmark, though I see the benefit of one employee board slot (see Proposal Three).

Shareholders ought to have the right to nominate a slate of truly independent directors. Surely large institutional investors—above all pension funds—would be eager to put forward the highest-quality individuals who would help to maximize company performance. If senior managers also happen to be major shareholders of a company, they would be free to vote their shares for board candidates of their choice as well.

The goal is not to create an adversarial relationship between the board and management. It is to create real accountability and fresh insight.

Bill George, the former CEO and chairman of Medtronic, a manufacturer of medical devices, can attest to the value of a strong and independent board. Under his leadership in the mid-1990s, eleven of twelve directors approved a proposed $2.5 billion takeover of Alza, a maker of drug-delivery systems.[30] The lone holdout director, an executive at a pharmaceutical company, pressed his case with George after the board meeting, arguing that the acquisition would lead Medtronic astray from its core market into sales channels where it had little experience. The CEO realized the gravity of the risk and reconvened the board on a telephone conference. The other members of the board agreed that although the deal made financial sense, it might take the company off-course, and they rescinded their decision. George knows how rare it is for a director to hold ground on an unpopular position, yet wants to encourage the practice on his board: "Later, I told [the dissenting director] how much I admired his courage and willingness to stand against the board."[31]

Proposal Two: Split the Role of CEO and Chairman

Boards tend to do their best when a nonexecutive chairman rules the agenda. It is too tempting for the CEO to turn board meetings into a pep rally. A division of responsibilities also provides the board with more authority to act, in practical terms if not psychologically.

Wintrust Financial Corporation, a financial services holding company headquartered in Lake Forest, Illinois, with assets in excess of $3.2 billion, represents an effective governance model. When it replaced its CEO in 1998, the board elected to place an independent director, John Lillard, in the chairman's post. The new CEO and former president, Edward Wehmer, admits that he held low expectations for how effective it would be to share power with Lillard, then age seventy-two, a retired investment management executive: "I wasn't going to hang around to be No. 2 [again]. You can't have a company with two leaders."[32]

The forty-eight-year-old Wehmer agreed to the arrangement, with the stipulation that Lillard maintain his office away from company headquarters. Lillard runs Wintrust's board meetings, and he introduced separate executive sessions with other independent members of the board. Early in 2002, he made a key introduction that led Wehmer to make a substantial acquisition of another financial holding company. Four years into the relationship, Wehmer has been pleasantly surprised at how well splitting the roles of CEO and chairman has worked out. Lillard shares that the secret is to lead quietly and let the CEO manage.[33]

Proposal Three: Put Someone on the Board Who Really Has a Lot to Lose

When major companies collapse, rank-and-file employees usually turn out to be the biggest losers. Their jobs disappear, and their pension funds sink. Who better than an employee to practice vigorous oversight of the company's operations? Besides, an employee would offer other directors a ground-floor perspective on what's really happening.

The employee representative should not be selected by the CEO, a method sure to bring in prized lap dogs. The entire workforce could participate in an electoral process every three years to put forward the individual they consider best able to promote their interests on the board.

Proposal Four: Trust But Verify

It is a good idea for directors to meet periodically without management present in order to air honest opinions and doubts. Even setting aside the last half-hour of a board meeting for a directors-only session could prove to be valuable. Directors also would be wise to have their own financial and legal advisers (not those used by the company) when management asks them to consider a major move, like a merger.

Above all, directors would be well served to establish an open line to operation managers throughout the company. Very few directors are privy to independent verification and frank conversation. Executives may find this practice unsettling; they would prefer to filter the flow of information that reaches directors.

The U.S. retail giant Target has set a pace that other companies would do well to match. Ten of the company's eleven directors are free from any other ties to the company, and CEO Robert Ulrich encourages them to communicate directly with other company managers without passing first through his office.[34]

Proposal Five: Raise the Stakes

Nothing promotes hearty vigilance like an economic stake. At least half of a director's compensation should be paid in shares or options that he or she cannot sell until twelve months after leaving the board. Some companies require directors to buy company stock as an entry fee. In either case, the intention is to build director equity.

Proposal Six: Rotate the Wheel

A business enterprise is not well served by a firmly entrenched board. Becoming a director should not be the equal of an appointment to the Supreme Court, with lifetime tenure. Following are some appropriate term limits:

○ Reelection every three years

○ No more than three consecutive terms

○ Mandatory retirement at the age of seventy

○ Service on a maximum of three corporate boards at any one time

Proposal Seven: Let Democracy Rule

Shareholders deserve to have more influence on how their companies are governed. The vast majority of corporations require a supermajority of anywhere from 60 to 80 percent of total shares outstanding to alter a company's bylaws. That's almost an impossible threshold to cross.

At Bristol-Myers Squibb, for example, a shareholder resolution to hold annual elections for board directors has won a majority of votes cast for six consecutive years, including a tally of 69 percent of votes cast in 2002. But the company has ignored the results because the resolution has fallen short of the firm's required supermajority (as a percentage of shares outstanding, the resolution won only 46 percent).[35]

"Despite more than 200 years of political practice in the United States, democracy remains an ideology strangely alien to many corporate boardrooms," declared maverick board director Walter Hewlett.[36] Whether Hewlett was right about opposing his company's merger with Compaq remains to be seen. But his critique of the closed, autocratic structure of corporate boards is dead-on.

Here's a modest proposal: shareholder resolutions that pass by 60 percent of the shares cast for two consecutive years should be binding.

The Way to Wealth

"A little neglect may breed mischief: for want of a nail the shoe was lost; for want of a shoe the horse was lost; and for want of a horse the rider was lost."[37] Not that long ago, Benjamin Franklin's homespun wisdom seemed quaint; all of a sudden, it strikes us as deeply profound. Maybe that's because we yearn to get back to basics: a respect for fair value and the value of fairness.

Charlie Johnson can attest to the lasting appeal of Franklin's philosophy. Charlie today is the chairman and chief executive of Franklin Resources, one of the globe's premier investment companies, with roughly $250 billion total assets under management.[38]

Back in 1947, Charlie's father started Franklin, naming the company in honor of the early American revolutionary who penned *The Way to Wealth*. Charlie joined the firm in 1957 as a broker and took over the business when his father retired. He recalls that most people at that time did not even know what a mutual fund was. Today, of course, mutual funds are the savings vehicle of choice in the United States.

Charlie built Franklin's business in a manner that would have pleased Ben. For over twenty-five years, he signed every company check and approved every invoice, from covering payroll and office supplies to investments. "It's worthwhile to look over a P&L [profit and loss] statement, but it's quite another thing to know where your cash is going," says Charlie. Franklin eventually outgrew his capacity to maintain his one-man financial oversight. But Charlie continues to run a tight ship, reminding his managers that the company wins not by making money off customers but by making money for them.

Charlie is not as concerned as I am about the integrity of the market today, yet I listen carefully to his point of view. He has notched nearly fifty profitable years in the investment business and has watched the tide of corporate scandals ebb and flow. "We have good systems of accountability in place," he declares confidently, "and they eventually catch up with crooked business operations and dishonest managers."

But truth be known, Charlie puts his confidence in the long haul, not in quick turnarounds. His memo to investors in Franklin's 2001 annual report ought to be placed on the desk of every leader who has the task and responsibility to govern a corporation: "Although we have no control over many short-term factors that affect investment returns, we know that over the long term, discipline and consistency will prove rewarding."[39]

Transparency is the hallmark of a consistent enterprise. Firms that present truthful information, operate openly, and stand behind their word make our risks feel calculated. Let's turn our attention now to the essential steps for building a transparent company.

Chapter Two

Transparency and Integrity

Principle Two

A company's business operations will be transparent
to shareholders, employees, and the public, and
its executives will stand by the integrity of their
decisions.

Vital Signs

Does the company provide clear reports of its assets and operations? Are financial reports verified by auditors who are free
of conflict of interest in the company? Do corporate directors
diligently monitor and verify management reports? Do workers have open and ready access to financial records? Are the
rationale and assumptions behind accounting practices transparent? Does the company consistently provide accurate
information on failed business ventures, as well as realistic

appraisals of anticipated successes? Are off-the-balance-sheet transactions reported? Are detailed reports on cash flow provided? Are clear lines of corporate decision making established? Does the company stand behind its contractual obligations? Do senior executives trust their employees to make decisions? Are mistakes covered up or openly admitted?

I have operated in international financial markets wearing lots of different hats. I started an economic development agency in the early 1980s focused on the rural poor of Latin America, covered global business trends as a journalist, and handled international deals for a niche investment bank in the technology sector. So whenever I hear a business manager speak glibly of taking the company global, I shudder. Over the years, I have witnessed an array of U.S. and European enterprises stumble in underdeveloped markets because they get lost in a quagmire of shady capitalism.

In Latin America, for example, I found that managers regularly misrepresent to investors the truth about their assets, their liabilities, and their profits. Local business operators win favor by exploiting their close connections to political power and, not infrequently, run roughshod over legal structures and worker rights. Revenues on the books mysteriously slide into the elusive margins of business operations, and the periodic, almost inevitable, exposé of improper behavior soils the company's reputation back in the home market.

Now these same practices are surfacing closer to home. At first, we treated Enron as the saga of one failed company. Once the ranks of the club started to swell with Tyco, WorldCom,

Adelphia, Waste Management, and Global Crossing, all the signs started to point to a rotten system.

The crooked path runs beyond the corporation's doors. Outside professionals who once took great pride in the honesty and integrity of their work spin their own web of deception. Auditors look the other way so that their firms can rake in millions of dollars from higher-margin consulting work. Securities analysts mislead investors in order to pump up banking fees; storied brokerage firm Merrill Lynch privately called stocks "dogs" and "pieces of junk" while telling the public to "accumulate" and "buy."[1] The attitude that only wimps tell the truth and play by the rules is perversely pervasive.

I left *Business 2.0* magazine to take on the CEO role at a technology start-up in Silicon Valley. I will share the saga of that company more fully in the final chapter, but note one incident here. My search for early-stage capital led me at one point to Salomon Smith Barney, an investment bank that was wildly successful during the telecommunications boom of the late 1990s. A friend introduced me to Rick Olson, who handled the private wealth management of a number of America's top telecom CEOs, including Bernie Ebbers, Joseph Nacchio, and Stephen Garofalo.

My company was still at too early a stage for Salomon, but Olson expressed some interest in tracking our development. He offered to introduce me—as long as our venture made steady progress—to his high-profile clients, who always were looking for an up-and-coming player in the telecom sector.

No doubt to impress me with the leverage that Salomon could offer in the market, Olson ran me through some of the initial public offerings (IPOs) Salomon had led. He gloated about the shares that his firm had allocated to clients at prices ridiculously low given the heights to which the stock soared.

Allegations are now surfacing from ex-Salomon employees that Olson, along with his close associate Jack Grubman, rewarded top executives with hot IPO stocks for business their companies gave to the firm (or might give to it in the future).[2] In some cases, Salomon allegedly gave telecom executives allocations at a stock's initial offering price even days after the shares had been trading substantially higher in the open market. It would be hard to find a lower-risk model for investing. According to an ex-Salomon broker who worked with Olson, other Salomon clients were not afforded the same opportunity.

Olson did not tell me anything that I could construe as illegal. All the same, I recall walking out of his office in Los Angeles that day with a sinking feeling that capital markets are rigged unfairly for the benefit of insiders as never before.

Transparency: Why It Is So Important

This chapter focuses on transparency—that is, operating with complete candor and integrity so that things can be seen for what they truly are. I feature four essential steps for building a transparent company:

Step One: Establish a transparent culture.

Step Two: Practice transparent management.

Step Three: Deliver transparent financials.

Step Four: Make transparent commitments (and stand behind them).

Transparency is fundamental to business enterprises. Investors need to be confident that reported profits are real, that executives won't use their posts to enrich themselves, and that systems of accountability are in place to expose and punish abuses. Workers have to believe in a company's commitment to build value if they are to put their careers, and the security of their families, into its hands. Customers assume the integrity of the transaction; once that trust is broken, they rarely give the company a second chance. In the absence of transparency, all of these relationships are at risk.

Enron betrayed all conventions of transparency. Investigations reveal that executives set up thousands of affiliate companies to hide their financial shenanigans. Enron sold its own assets like pipelines and power plants to the affiliates and booked the proceeds as income. The affiliates, in turn, raised funds to relieve Enron of its debt. These transactions appeared on the financial statement as a tidy double dip: positive revenues and reduced debt. Enron employees now confess that they were given incentives for finding creative ways to pull off the sales of such assets; the more lucrative the transaction was, the higher was the bonus.[3]

It's an irony, then, that my first model of transparent management comes out of Enron.

STEP ONE: ESTABLISH A TRANSPARENT CULTURE

Back in 1994, Jim Alexander arrived at Enron, persuaded like just about everyone else in Houston that it was a company on the move.[4] His initial assignment was to set up Enron Global Power and Pipelines as a publicly traded affiliate to keep high-debt assets off Enron's balance sheet. Jim initially served as Global Power's chief financial officer and then president.

The Canary in the Coal Mine

Generally, a corporation is barred from basing its profits on sales to a subsidiary, but Enron's accounting firm, Arthur Andersen, and its principal law firm, Vinson & Ellkins, worked closely with the company to push the boundaries. In brief, they drew up a corporate structure that gave Enron a 52 percent equity share of Global Power, enough of a separation to allow Enron to count transactions between the two entities as income.

Despite the appearance of independence, outside investors should have seen a red flag in the prospectus for Global Power's initial public offering: "Enron will control the company and will have extensive ongoing relationships with the company. Certain conflicts of interest exist and may arise in the future as a result of these partnerships."

It did not take long for those conflicts of interest to surface. Enron told Global Power to make transactions that were to its own benefit regardless of the impact on Global Power's balance sheet. Jim Alexander believed it was his obligation as an executive officer to guard the interests of Global Power's non-Enron shareholders, however. A committee of independent directors had ultimate responsibility for vetting transactions between Enron and Global Power. Unfortunately, they were not so conscientious.

Often it is hard to know absolutely for sure whether your company is acting with impropriety. Every doubt you harbor meets a justification from colleagues who defend the practice.

So what alerted Jim to possible malfeasance? "I consider whether I would feel proud or ashamed if a report on our actions reached the front page of every major newspaper in the country," he replies resolutely. After a moment's pause, he adds: "Maybe the best sign that you are in danger is when someone says, 'Everyone does it.' When you begin saying that to yourself, you know you're in it deep."

Jim decided not to play along. Once it became clear that it was not in Global Power's interests to execute the deals that Enron proposed, he tried to influence other key decision makers internally. When that failed, he shared his concerns with Richard Kinder, Enron's corporate president at the time. Jim recalls that Kinder was less than sympathetic, shouting at him repeatedly over the course of an hour-long discussion: "Me! My! That's the problem with this company—everybody's saying 'Me! My!'" On other occasions, Enron executives put it more bluntly to Jim's subordinates: "You guys better take your Global Power hat off and put on your Enron hat."

Jim even sounded the alarm to Enron chairman Kenneth Lay. He informed Lay of his concerns about Global Power as well as other irregularities he had observed at Enron, including dubious accounting practices some managers were using to manipulate the financial results for their units. Once again, Jim's message fell on deaf ears. The meeting lasted all of fifteen minutes and ended with Lay's promising weakly to raise the issues with Kinder.

Feeling that he had reached a dead end, Jim resigned from Global Power in October 1995. It would take another six years or so for the house of cards at Enron to tumble. Jim's story shows that corrupt cultures do not grow overnight. As he puts it, "We were the dead canary in the coal mine."

By the end of the 1990s, Enron executives took more control of its affiliates, usually placing its own people at the helm. Obviously, Enron executives did not want gatekeepers with conscience around who would hold the company accountable to sound business practices.

Transparency Flows from Deep Reserves

Although Jim Alexander left Global Power with a bitter taste in his mouth, he did not lose his faith in private enterprise. He teamed up with a trusted partner in Roger Jarvis, the former CEO of King Ranch (the parent company of King Ranch Oil & Gas Co).[5] The two partners launched Spinnaker Exploration in 1996. Based in Houston, Spinnaker operates as a pure exploration company searching for crude oil and natural gas reserves, primarily in the Gulf of Mexico. The firm today is one of the highest-valued companies in the oil and natural gas exploration sector, with a market cap over $1 billion, $200 million cash in the bank, and zero debt.

From the start, Jim and Roger made transparency a core value infusing all of Spinnaker's operations. Jim had seen first-hand at Enron that a corrupt culture rots a corporation to its core. "You can talk about valuable assets in strictly financial terms, but at the end of the day, the company culture is what you're all about," he stresses.

The Spinnaker executives realized that building a responsible corporate culture depends in no small part on hiring and retaining the right people. So when making their early key hiring decisions, they set a high standard: someone they personally trusted had to vouch for a candidate's integrity.

Jim and Roger were looking for partners, not merely salaried employees, to help them develop their business. They gave more than lip-service to that philosophy. When they launched the company, both men invested their own money alongside outside venture capital. They then offered the same terms of investment to the first thirty employees whom they brought into the company. Actually, they went one step further: making an investment in the company, though not in any fixed amount, was a condition for being hired.

"We ran the job interviews with the same tone and message we used in presenting to investors," recalls Roger. He and Jim wanted prospective employees to know clearly the risks, hurdles, and opportunities facing the company. Interviewees were told that they were not likely to see a rise in their base salaries and that the company was aiming to be a long-term success, not a shooting rocket. "As funny as it sounds, we were inviting them to pay us to get a job that would compensate them less than their existing job," says Roger with a chuckle.

Once their team was in place, Jim and Roger made sure that fresh air would reach every corner of their new company. Every Monday morning, Spinnaker executives hold an all-hands-on-deck meeting with employees. They share reports on financial operations, investments, unit reorganizations and expansions, and just about any other state of corporate affairs. The only exception occurs when the company is involved in sensitive negotiations, and confidentiality takes strategic, if not legal, priority—the details of an acquisition, for example.

Roger admits that he was nervous at first about sharing sensitive data with employees that might find their way outside of the company. "But we've never had any problems; when workers are treated like partners, interests become aligned."

If the managers who lead the company do not tell the truth to their employees, deception cascades throughout the company. Employees will lie back to managers and to each other. "Once you stop telling the truth, you spend as much of your time covering up for your lies as you do creating real value," Jim warns.

Spinnaker's open communication is quite impressive. All the same, employees measure their leaders by actions more than words. Jim admits that employees were convinced of the leadership's sincerity once they made key corporate decisions that backed up their promises. On one occasion, for example, they were very close to a merger deal that would have been financially advantageous to Spinnaker. But the new management team that they would have brought in-house, and expected some of their own people to work for, practiced a highly autocratic and close-lipped style of leadership. Spinnaker executives passed on the deal. "That sent a strong message to our team how much we valued our culture," says Jim.

Spinnaker executives practice transparency with their investors as well. Although their firm has experienced spectacular growth, they refuse to hire an investor relations firm. "We don't want anyone standing between us and our shareholders massaging a message,"

How to Build Transparency into Your Corporate DNA

o Hire the right employees, and prepare them for excellence.

o Do not tolerate deception.

o Share openly the state of all internal operations.

o Make decisions that support company commitments.

o Capitalize the business appropriately.

o Make realistic revenue projections, and communicate the rationale for those projections.

o Provide full disclosure to investors.

o Don't take shortcuts; develop the business with a long-term approach.

explains Roger. He is convinced that investors can do more good for the company when they know exactly how the company is performing.

Jim underscores the importance of capitalizing a company appropriately. Echoing the sentiments of Gary Erickson (featured in Chapter One), Jim believes that too many companies make unrealistic income projections to attract investors. "Most companies overpromise and underperform, then make up the difference by lying," says Jim with dry wit.

Jim and Roger did not want to fall into that habit. They honestly explained to their investors from the start that Spinnaker operates in a commodities market where revenues ebb and flow. Investors should expect volatility from quarter to quarter. After six years, the company has yet to make an acquisition and diligently reports realistic numbers to shareholders. Not surprisingly, it attracts investors who reward candor along with performance.

Roger still serves today as CEO and chairman of the board of directors. After four years of leadership, Jim has removed himself gracefully from the pressure cooker of building a start-up to pursue his personal interests in religious ministry. Yet he leaves behind a strong testament to the very practice Enron executives worked so ardently to avoid: a bedrock of transparency.

Step Two: Practice Transparent Management

Every company wants its employees to think and act like owners. Generously distributing equity certainly helps, but by itself it is not enough. Workers do not truly take ownership of a company until they are included in meaningful decisions that shape the direction of the business.

Danny Grossman, the founder and CEO of Wild Planet Toys, a designer and manufacturer of imaginative toys headquartered in San Francisco, is convinced that transparent management makes the difference.[6] Danny launched Wild Planet in 1993, and the company has enjoyed solid growth ever since. Its revenues have grown 50 percent annually to go along with steadily rising profitability. Despite the dizzying pace, Danny takes the time to nurture an open community.

In the corporate world, employees are not always clear why decisions are made and who will ultimately take responsibility for their execution. At times, the management team can come across as a secret society. To counter that dynamic, Danny aims to illuminate the process behind each major decision and what role, if any, his employees will have in shaping it. He admits that he adopted this leadership style to compensate for his own weakness: "I like to hear from all quarters and arrive at consensus," he shares. "But at the same time, I have a tendency to move toward what I want in a passive-aggressive way."

To make the management process at Wild Planet more transparent, Danny designed a code to signal distinct modes of decision making. Whenever a major decision arises, senior managers share explicitly with their subordinates that any one of four modes will be followed: a tombstone, a boulder, a stake, and a notion. The code requires some explaining.

When a *tombstone* is invoked, a senior manager makes the decision with little input from colleagues. If an executive is going to lay down a tombstone, it's best to name the nonnegotiables straight up so that everyone in the company can deal with it on that basis. Although this mode is rarely deployed at Wild Planet, Danny admits he is not afraid to act solo when a core company value is at stake. "Although I like consensus, we don't pretend to be democratic. It would be dishonest to pretend the majority rules because the reality is that some people have more power than others, and at different times," he explains.

More commonly, the company is confronted with a *boulder,* and moving it out of the way necessitates strong collaboration. A senior manager will make the decision but first will give colleagues a fair hearing and engage in serious dialogue.

At yet other times, management feels it is important for as many employees as possible to have a *stake* in a decision process, and that points to a consensus model. High participation is solicited, for instance, on matters of company branding, outsourcing production overseas, or creating the best distribution channels for products. There may be workers who find fault with the final decision, of course, but they nonetheless feel as if they had their input.

A *notion* mode is typically used in the early stages of a decision process, or perhaps even before it's clear how a decision should be made. The aim is to stimulate creative ideas that will help to address a problem.

Danny extols the psychic rewards that employees gain when they work for a company that practices transparent management. As evidence, he points to

---

Four Modes of Decision Making: Wild Planet's Code

- Tombstone: decision by mandate

- Boulder: consultation invited

- Stake: maximum ownership of the idea is goal

- Notion: brainstorming time

the challenge of building a toy company on the home turf of Silicon Valley during the height of the Internet boom (Wild Planet shared its office building with several Internet companies). Danny could not compete on the basis of salaries or stock options, yet he did not lose one employee to a dot-com company. That happened, he claims, because employees trust the way decisions are made and know how their job relates to the company's overall performance.

STEP THREE: DELIVER TRANSPARENT FINANCIALS

How companies book their sales has never before mattered so much to investors. Even blue-chip companies like Coca-Cola, Merck, and Xerox have soiled their reputations in recent years with sloppy, if not fraudulent, accounting.[7] In one glaring case, the SEC filed suit against Waste Management executives for inflating reported profits using accounting tricks that allowed the company to mask almost $1.7 billion in expenses during a five-year period in the 1990s.[8]

The tech economy perfected the art of financial sleight-of-hand. At the height of the Internet economy, I looked under the hood of more than one dot-com wonder only to discover that a big chunk of their reported income was in fact barter revenue—a sales swap between companies for advertising or other services that offered no real incremental value to earnings.

I also bumped into a more sophisticated trade illusion called the roundtripper. Here's how it works: Company A pays out $250 million in amorphous units of, say, broadband to Company B. After some time, Company B floats broadband back to Company A in—surprise!—exactly $250 million worth of units.

Both companies then book $250 million as revenue on their income statements.

Clearly, the system for financial reporting has broken down, yet no one wants to take responsibility for the wonky numbers. The board of directors points an accusing finger at management, management blames the auditor, and the auditor claims that both management and the board did not make the adjustments it recommended. Frankly, there's plenty of blame to pass around. If misrepresentations are indeed taking place, all parties are obligated to disclose the error and restate earnings, not simply gloss over the faulty statements with what they refer to as "adjustments."

While shareholders hope for transparency from management, they rely on external auditors to hold them accountable to the numbers they report. In theory, an auditor's signature on a corporate report should bear witness to an accurate account of company performance. But conflicts of interest now cast a cloud of suspicion over the accounting process. In the witty repose of Paul O'Neil, an auditor's endorsement may mean only that a company has "cooked the books to generally accepted standards."[9]

No simple formula will magically plug up all the leaks in corporate accounting and reporting. Nonetheless, a single company can take decisive action to enhance the transparency of its financial operations. I offer six specific practices that are both broad-based and realistic:

○ *Mix auditing and consulting from the same firm with caution.* Bad accounting is usually not accidental; it is symptomatic. For two decades, lucrative consulting contracts have dwarfed the income that accounting firms could generate from more traditional services. The heightened focus on consulting revenue caused some firms to trample on long-honored standards. "You know the financial reporting system is in trouble when accountants stop digging deep into the books because it might endanger their own fee-driven bottom line," stresses Dominic Tarantino, a forty-one-year veteran and one-time world chairman of Pricewaterhouse.[10]

Petro-Canada, one of Canada's largest oil and gas companies, disclosed that it paid more than $5 million to Arthur Andersen in 2001. But only a small portion of that bill—$711,000, or about 14 percent—was for the company's external audit. The rest was paid out for an internal audit. Responding to shareholders' concerns about this conflict of interest, Petro-Canada's management changed its course: its external auditor will no longer conduct its internal audit as well.[11] A company committed to transparency should follow suit.

○ *Make accounting assumptions clear.* There are many ways to write off expenses, such as depreciation and deferred costs. Financial managers should take care to illuminate the logic behind a firm's chosen practice. In that spirit, auditors ought to inform shareholders whenever a company is adopting aggressive, even if arguably legal, reporting to improve its top-line numbers. The goal is not strict adherence to any given set of rules but to present investors with a lucid picture.

○ *Track real earnings.* Shareholders have a right to know if a company's earnings are being buttressed by an acquisition, including off-the-balance-sheet transactions. Acquisitions should not be allowed to mask a deficiency in corporate sales (see the related discussion on acquisitions and earnings in Chapter One).

○ *Detail the cash flow.* Most financial statements include a statement of cash flow. That figure, however, is typically so undefined it does not provide insight into the actual state of business operations. More detailed maps of the cash flow—by major transaction, by division, by plant—make it harder to overlook, or hide, problem areas in the company.

○ *Switch auditors every seven years.* Rotating audit firms periodically would minimize entrenched conflicts of interest. In the United States at the moment, only the senior auditor on an account must depart after seven years. I favor a complete rotation of firms.

Some proponents of reform (and U.S. lawmakers) advocate for shorter rotation cycles of five years or less. Although I see the wisdom of rotation, accelerated cycles have their drawbacks. Rotation results in the loss of valuable cumulative knowledge about accounting operations and internal control systems of a particular client, and to a lesser degree a particular industry. That's largely why audit failures are three times more prevalent in the first two years of a client relationship.[12]

○ *Encourage and reward honesty, starting at the top of the corporate ladder.* Financial corruption usually starts at the top of the corporate ladder, says Arthur Brief, a business professor at Tulane University, who studies how managers apply their values to financial reporting. Brief found that 47 percent of nearly four hundred executives he surveyed were willing to commit fraud by understating write-offs that would cut into their companies' profits.[13]

Once top managers start playing games with the numbers, honesty becomes sparse all the way down the chain of command. Brief's research shows that most nonmanagement workers are willing to go along with fraud if it means pleasing their boss. "People in subordinate roles will comply with their superiors even when that includes wrongdoing that goes against their individual moral code," he says.

Senior managers who commit major fraud usually do not begin with that intention. They start off cutting small corners, and the need to cover up these indiscretions often leads to more serious deceptions. If the practices I recommend are implemented, however, and an active audit committee is in place to monitor the accounting process, there will be less opportunity and less temptation.

No set of accounting mechanisms can overcome moral lapses, unfortunately. The transparent corporation relies on managers with integrity—leaders who can speak plainly about what the company has, and has not, achieved.

At the funeral of the original Arthur Andersen (who must be turning in his grave to see what the future hath wrought), the presiding minister spoke eloquently to what moral leadership looks like in the world of business: "What did Mr. Andersen stand for? What was the guiding principle of his life? To me he stands as a representative of principles as opposed to expediency. . . . He could not be bought with money, but, what is more important he could not be bought with power, influence, prestige, or social position. And few, if any, were the people who could mislead him. He had the insight to see through subterfuge."[14]

How many of us in the business world might expect a similar eulogy to be delivered at our funeral? Never forget: Character charts our destiny (Heraclitus).

STEP FOUR: MAKE TRANSPARENT COMMITMENTS (AND STAND BEHIND THEM)

Granted, the odd individual can act with integrity, but is it really possible to build integrity into the ethos of the company? Southwest Airlines proves it is. "If one of our employees commits Southwest Airlines to doing something, we stand behind that commitment," chairman Herb Kelleher once declared. Company manager Bob Montgomery can testify that this promise is more than rhetoric.[15]

In the late 1970s, Bob started working at Southwest part-time on the baggage ramp. He became a jack-of-all-trades at the airline, serving as a ticket agent and a manager of customer service, and he took on several posts in business operations. By the mid-1980s, Southwest had grown well beyond its Dallas-Houston hub and was looking for someone to represent it before a national network of airports. Bob had the ideal background and was promoted to the position.

Bob's first test took place in Austin, Texas. The city's major airport at the time was situated only ten minutes from the state capitol. The airport was hemmed in by local neighborhoods, making expansion almost impossible. To meet a growing demand for air travel, Austin city officials elected to build a new airport and selected a locale situated far outside city limits.

Bob promised city officials that Southwest would support the new airport project and would contribute handsomely to preplanning costs. He brought the Austin proposal back to corporate headquarters, and Southwest executives duly signed the agreement.

It didn't take Bob long to realize that he had goofed. The proposed site for the airport was an hour's drive from downtown Austin and clearly a bad choice. The primary competitor to an airline that focuses on short-haul flights is the automobile, and Austin is a drivable distance to both Houston and Dallas. Common sense eventually won out, and a new airport eventually was built at a site much closer to the city.

Over a year passed before Bob had the chance to review his poor judgment with Kelleher. Flying on a plane together after an out-of-state meeting, Bob asked Kelleher the question that had burned his conscience: "Herb, do you remember that deal in Austin?"

"Oh yes, I remember that well," Kelleher said.

"You know as well as I did that it was a bone-headed deal and probably ended up costing the company up to half a million dollars," Bob spoke frankly.

"Well, I'm glad you finally figured that out!" Kelleher said with a hearty laugh.

Relieved to get his confession out of the way, Bob then aimed to satisfy his curiosity: "So, Herb, why did you sign that deal?"

"Because you gave your word," Kelleher answered resolutely.

The Southwest chairman went on to describe how, upon receiving the Austin proposal, the management team quickly recognized its shortcomings and prepared to deny the proposal. But after further inquiry, Kelleher learned that Bob had made an oral commitment to Austin city officials. "If Bob gave his word that we would support the deal, then that's what we're going to do," Herb said to his fellow executives, and the Austin deal was sealed.

How remarkable for a corporation to stand behind an oral agreement made by a midlevel manager. Absent a signed contract, imagine the wriggle room a team of corporate lawyers could exploit!

Maybe it is even more amazing that the company did not make Bob pay dearly for his mistake. As he has moved along in his career, Bob has compared his experience with friends who mess up on the job at other corporations. "They are humiliated, demoted, even fired for making a mistake," he says. The backing he received contributed to his growth into a company leader.

Now a vice president in charge of the construction and maintenance of all Southwest facilities nationwide, Bob is asked to make even more promises, and he carries on Kelleher's principles. He made a commitment to airport owners in Norfolk, Virginia, that Southwest would open a new terminal in October 2001. Then the tragic events of September 11 struck, leading to a nationwide airline shutdown and throwing the industry on its ear. Once the airports reopened, customers stayed away in droves. Nearly every U.S. carrier was forced to lay off workers and cut flights. Surely Southwest could not be blamed for delaying its entry into the Norfolk market, even if that meant hardship for the local airport, which it would. But Southwest opened as planned. "We had made a pledge that we would be up and running in October," says Bob matter-of-factly. "So instead of downsizing along with the rest of the industry, we stayed the course and honored our commitment."

Business transactions always involve some element of risk. A company can never be sure that a partner will stand behind its word. When a corporation builds the kind of reputation

Southwest has and is willing to back it up even in the face of adversity, partners line up to do business with them.

As the next chapter shows, a community yearns for corporate partners it can trust as well. When the firm does not stand behind its word, the community will hold it accountable.

Chapter Three

Community

Principle Three

A company will think of itself as part of a community
as well as a market.

Vital Signs

Has the company developed a strategic plan for its community investments? Do citizen concerns about the company's
impact get listened to and resolved? Does the company hire
locally at all levels of job classification? Are corporate
resources leveraged to advantage neighborhood networks? Are
employees actively encouraged to volunteer their skills and
experience to civic groups? Are local housing and educational
initiatives supported, especially those geared toward the eco-
nomically disadvantaged? Is consumer activity linked to tangible community benefits? Does the company contribute generously to the local tax base? Is economic activity initiated in
partnership with community groups? Are metrics used to

gauge the company's return on community investment? Are employees involved in the choice and development of community partnerships? Is a commitment in place to profit-share with the community?

Does the corporation have a moral obligation to the community? I think so, and my reason is simple. Companies use the natural resources, the labor, and the social infrastructure of a place to further their own private economic ends. It is small recompense to assist the community in improving its quality of life.

Many of my friends in the business world strongly disagree with my position. They argue that business best helps the community by focusing on profitability. When a firm succeeds, more jobs are created, more goods and services are offered, and the overall economy is boosted. Besides, they add, business executives have neither the experience nor the incentive to solve social problems. They should stick with what they know best: maximizing profits.

I remain unconvinced. Economic growth does not necessarily bring social progress. Historically, many business enterprises on their way to profit uprooted local populations, polluted the environment, and abused workers' rights. The single-minded pursuit of economic growth can exact a heavy toll on a community, I stress to my friends.

Despite the passion we bring to our positions, I wonder if our philosophical debate is becoming passé. The lines separating our positions are starting to blur. The corporation acts as a responsible vehicle for social good today as a condition for creating shareholder value. Business leaders who cannot figure out how to mesh their company's mission with the community's well-being may struggle to find profitability.

Two large U.S. corporations, Home Depot and Stanley Works, paid the price in 2002 for disregarding community expectations. A quick review of how these firms took their lumps, and why, points to the rising importance of corporate-community relations.

Not in My Backyard

In the civic elections of March 2002, the people of Mountain View, California, population seventy-six thousand, voted down Home Depot. Home Depot is not the first company to lose a ballot resolution blocking its entry into a local market, and it surely will not be the last. But the public debate leading up to its election loss ought to serve as a wake-up call for any major corporation.

The building supplies retailer was hoping to establish a 125,000-square foot store in Mountain View.[1] Grassroots community groups charged that the megastore would push mom-and-pop hardware stores out of business and overrun residential streets with shopper traffic and noisy delivery trucks. In its defense, Home Depot officials trumpeted the boost the store would bring to the town's tax base and the hundreds of jobs it would create for local residents.

These issues are not uncommon when big-box retailers propose to bring a new store to a small community. In fact, the Swedish furniture retailer IKEA was embroiled in a parallel election battle in the spring of 2002 in East Palo Alto, just five miles up the highway from Mountain View. IKEA was proposing to build a 300,000-square-foot store in East Palo Alto that would attract a steady stream of customers from San Francisco to San Jose.

Days before the election, I tuned into a popular northern California radio show that was hosting a preelection debate on the two ballot resolutions: Home Depot in Mountain View and IKEA in East Palo Alto.[2] Not surprisingly, the discussion focused on the residential impact of the proposed stores.

But one theme in particular tipped the balance of the debate. Several critics blasted Home Depot for being a poor neighbor. They cited the problems that an existing Home Depot megastore had brought to another northern California community and alleged that the corporation's response to neighborhood complaints was woefully inadequate. Several callers also weighed in on IKEA, but their tone was quite different. Although the same residential issues were noted, they depicted IKEA as a progressive company that cares about the community and offers handsome benefits to its workers.

The editors of the *San Jose Mercury News* echoed this message in its own pages. To explain why they opposed the ballot measure in Mountain View, the editors called attention to the high incidence of grievances against Home Depot in other towns and the corporation's "history of not responding to those complaints." Although the editors also opposed the IKEA measure due to traffic considerations, once again no slight was made of IKEA's reputation.[3]

On election day, Mountain View voters resoundingly defeated the Home Depot measure by two to one. IKEA emerged with a narrow victory.[4] Although other factors surely played a part in the election results, corporate reputation was a significant influence on voters. Whether IKEA is indeed a better corporate citizen than Home Depot is a matter for more detailed analysis and fervent debate. Referring back to my Introduction, it does seem clear that Home Depot's reputation failed to serve as a guardian for its brand.

The drama in Mountain View mirrors a new ethic that consumers everywhere are beginning to embrace: corporations will not thrive if they fail to serve the community.

THE CORPORATE BERMUDA TRIANGLE

Perhaps no greater disregard for the local community—and flaunting of corporate arrogance—could match the Bermuda tax scheme. A number of American companies are looking to register their charter offshore to avoid paying taxes. No one faults a company for trying to minimize its taxes using above-the-board deductions, but it is a whole different matter to slip and slide around the tax code and stiff communities to cover the tab for local infrastructure.

Offshore tax schemes entail a complicated subterfuge. A few years ago, I helped an Australian company investigate whether it should relocate its corporate headquarters to the United States. We asked a renowned business strategy firm to lay out our options. Our meeting had all the earmarks of the global economy. The American consultants advised the Aussie executives to set up unofficial headquarters in the United States but incorporate in Bermuda. That way, the Aussie company could earn the bulk of its revenue in the United States and hire highly qualified American professionals, yet avoid paying U.S. corporate taxes. As the consultants proudly drew flowcharts on the board showing how the money would flow smoothly across borders, I recall thinking, *I bet none of these guys have children in the public schools.* (The fact that my local school district had that very week cut busing due to a lack of public funds put it at the top of my mind.)

Stanley Works is the best known of the wannabe Bermudans. The idea seems anachronistic from the get-go; Stanley's bright yellow logo on screwdrivers and tape measurers is such a distinctive American brand. Added to that is that the firm has been an anchor tenant in the small Connecticut town of New Britain for nearly 160 years.

But at the annual shareholders' meeting in 2002, Stanley CEO John Trani raised the flag of Bermuda to save the company $30 million in taxes.[5] Under the proposal, Stanley's offices would not actually move to Bermuda; incorporating there requires only a mailing address. But Stanley would send to the tiny island nation all of the profits that it earns on overseas sales.

For reasons that are a bit more complex, Stanley also would become a corporate resident of Barbados, where it would funnel earnings that the company generates in the U.S. market. Once these earnings are diverted offshore, they can be invested tax free in overseas factories.[6] Stanley then could shift the bulk of its production offshore as well (about half of the company's products already are manufactured overseas).

At the annual meeting, a shareholder warned Stanley's CEO that his proposal would damage the company's reputation and lamented what he saw as a shift in the corporate ethos: "[Stanley] was known for years as a company with a heart." To that comment, Trani gruffly replied, "Our job is not to be popular," and went on to explain why Stanley needed to make these moves to remain competitive in global markets.[7]

Although Trani made a compelling business case for his proposal, it was drowned out by his apparent disregard for the people who would be affected by his plan. In effect, he became an emblem for corporate greed in the American public. "Stanley Works ought to change its name to Stanley Flees," wrote the editors of the *New York Times*.[8]

A member of Stanley's machinists' union also tapped into popular sentiment: "This is really about the future of the corporation in America. Are companies going to stay loyal to our country and grow jobs here, where they made their money? The notion that a stock price is the only measure of a company's value is shortsighted."[9]

Due to intense public pressure, Stanley eventually dropped its relocation plan. Not only did the company face strong opposition from community groups, labor unions, and the media, the public attention generated by Stanley's proposal motivated the U.S. Congress to bring forward legislation that would penalize companies that resort to offshore tax schemes.[10] Although it's hard to measure the long-term damage to Stanley's reputation, the black eye on the yellow logo certainly did not look pretty.

CONSUMERS SWITCH BRANDS TO COMMUNITY-ORIENTED COMPANIES

A substantial body of market research shows the importance of a firm's community engagement to the consumer. Aging boomers and youth alike are attracted to the dual proposition that they can buy quality products and make the world a better place. A Cone/Roper consumer survey finds that two-thirds of American consumers will switch brands to reward community-oriented companies.[11] Similar trends are reported internationally. A high percentage of consumers in the United Kingdom

(86 percent), Italy (75 percent), and Australia (73 percent) claim they are more likely to support a company if it contributes to the social good.[12]

This data reinforce how critical it is for a company to develop a strategic plan for community engagement. Over the rest of this chapter, I do an in-depth feature on three of the best practices that I have run across in the corporate world. The examples represent three different models of corporate engagement: employee volunteering, community investment, and community at the core. These models are neither mutually exclusive nor exhaustive. The needs of the local community and the passion of those who initiate action within the firm will determine the best course of action. What does matter, though, is the sincerity and depth of a firm's commitment.

Charitable giving, for instance, ought to be treated as a baby step in a company's community engagement. Yes, philanthropy provides valuable funding for nonprofit groups that are attending to social needs. On its own, however, charity does not make a company a player in a community network.

Consumers are cynical about the motives behind corporate charity. In a Hill & Knowlton survey of American consumers, three out of four people say that companies participate in philanthropic activities to gain good publicity. Less than a quarter of those surveyed believe that companies make charitable gifts because they are truly committed to a community cause.[13]

On the other end of the spectrum, some corporations address thorny social problems as a potential business opportunity. Ahold, a global food retailer headquartered in the Netherlands with nearly $75 billion annually in sales, has pioneered several such initiatives in Europe.[14] Grocery stores worldwide find it tough to operate profitably in low-income

Moving the Company into the Community: How Deep Do You Go?

Charitable giving: periodic support given to a wide range of community groups

Cause-related marketing: marketing goods and services in partnership with community-based organizations

Employee volunteering: structured programs that encourage workers to get involved in community projects

Community investment: direct corporate resources devoted to community improvement

Community at the core: involving the community in virtually every aspect of the operation, from profit sharing to hiring to marketing

urban zones. But Ahold boldly concocted a novel business model in a municipality of the Dutch industrial town of Enschede. The grocery retailer developed an alliance between local government and nine other companies (including fast-food giant McDonalds and Rabobank, a major European bank) to generate a critical mass of commercial activity. The coalition also set up a recovery program for drug addicts, who were responsible for the bulk of the crime in urban Enschede. Designed to help addicts integrate back into society, the rehab program over time led to a reduction in local crime. In sum, the corporate-community cooperation created a viable environment for business activity, a feat neither Ahold nor its partners could have achieved acting alone.

The most innovative corporations like Ahold favor long-term projects that earn them a credible stake in the communities where they operate. They plan out a community investment strategy that maximizes the impact of their donated money, volunteer time, influence, and management expertise. In return for their commitment, they develop a reserve of social capital that turns out to be invaluable in watershed moments. Corporations could avoid much government regulation and civic opposition, like Home Depot faced in Mountain View, if they addressed community concerns and expectations well before they become politicized.

EMPLOYEE VOLUNTEERING:
THE TIMBERLAND COMPANY

Timberland, headquartered in Stratham, New Hampshire, incorporates community service into practically everything it does. The footwear and apparel company even reports the results of its good deeds along with the financials each quarter. That's a lot of good news to share: the company generated over $1 billion in sales and returned $112 million in profit in 2001.[15]

The seeds of volunteerism were planted at Timberland in 1989 when a small group from Boston called City Year requested fifty pairs of Timberland boots for its youth service organization. City Year espoused a grand dream to make voluntary community service accessible to all of America's youth. Moved by their enthusiasm, Timberland's chief executive, Jeffrey Swartz, donated the boots and visited one of City Year's community projects. He returned with a vision for turning his own company into a potent force for social change.

Timberland launched an in-house volunteer program in 1992, the Path of Service. The program gave employees sixteen hours of paid time each year to volunteer during regular work hours. Due to strong employee participation, the program expanded to thirty-two hours of paid leave in 1995 and then forty hours in 1997, where it remains today.

Workers are given a lot of flexibility to choose their own volunteer activities. Service can range from serving meals in a homeless shelter to coaching a Little League baseball team. Above all, the company wants to make it as easy as possible for workers to find a service program that matches their interests. It's effective: more than 90 percent of Timberland workers take part in the Path of Service.

The company added another dimension to the Path of Service in 2001 when it formed a service sabbatical program. Up to four employees each year are awarded three to six months of leave to work full time with a nonprofit organization of their choosing. The sabbatical comes with full pay and benefits, and participating employees return to their same job after completing their assignment.

Although community well-being ranks high on Timberland's agenda, the Path of Service is first and foremost an avenue for employee enrichment. "We believe that investing in our community begins by investing in our employees," declares Swartz.

Total Volunteer Hours Served by Timberland Path of Service Employees

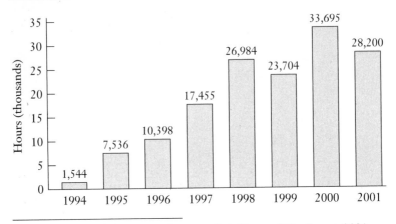

Source: Timberland Company, *Corporate Social Responsibility Report, 2001.*

The story of Maureen Franzosa, a merchandise analyst at Timberland, is evidence that helping workers to help their communities pays big dividends for everyone.

Making a Personal Contribution

Maureen volunteers at Sexual Assault Support Services (SASS), located in Portsmouth, New Hampshire.[16] The victim of sexual abuse typically is taken to a hospital for treatment and a rape kit evaluation, a clinical check that may be required for subsequent legal action. SASS volunteers to accompany the survivor through this difficult ordeal.

When Maureen started looking for a volunteer position, she was working full time at Timberland and parenting two teenage children. That combination left precious few spaces in her schedule. The on-call-at-home role of an SASS volunteer fit perfectly, and she started volunteering at SASS for three shifts a month of night duty.

Within a year, Maureen was intimately familiar with the prevalence of sexual abuse and the impact it wreaks on its survivors, and she wanted a chance to invest herself more fully in SASS. In her application form to the sabbatical program, Maureen passionately stated her case: "SASS's mission is an important one. The victims of these crimes are our friends, our neighbors, our children. Many victims are anonymous; they suffer in violence. I want to be a part of this mission."

Timberland selected Maureen to be the first recipient of a sabbatical: a six-month assignment. She expected to spend half her time continuing in direct support service to survivors of sexual abuse and the other half in school education.

Joining the education team was a new role for Maureen. SASS makes presentations in elementary schools, often using puppets to show complex situations

Making It Easy to Serve

Timberland workers can walk many pathways to volunteer:

○ A "service station" in the lobby at corporate headquarters to promote volunteer opportunities

○ Forty hours of paid service leave annually

○ Flexibility to accommodate the volunteer interests of individual workers

○ Team projects initiated by departments or informal bands of colleagues

○ An annual companywide day of service

○ Three- to six-month paid sabbaticals for voluntary service children might encounter and the choices they may have to make. During a session, they ask the kids to think about the grown-ups they can trust—whom they might go to if they were hurt or scared. The sessions also address the nuances of a secret—fun secrets like birthday surprises and a scary secret that an adult has told them not to share.

Looking back at her sabbatical, Maureen's memory often flips to a one-week period when she helped four children under the age of seven in separate incidents of abuse. "The parents would ask me, 'What could I have done?'" Maureen recalls. "I was glad to be there to reassure them that they did everything right. The most important thing they did was to listen and believe their child."

Although Maureen assumed her duties would be limited to education and direct service, an unexpected turn of events led to a few changes. Purely by coincidence, the day Maureen arrived to begin her sabbatical, the executive director of SASS resigned. In the next two months, five more permanent staff workers left for a variety of reasons. A staff of eight was suddenly down to three people.

The remaining staff did not have much experience in marketing, operations, and human resources. Maureen's corporate expertise in the for-profit world therefore became a huge asset. She secured additional help from Timberland's human resource department, who visited SASS and conducted a workshop on leadership and teamwork.

Nonprofit groups are typically underresourced, of course. Timberland's goal is to send out individuals who can supply nonprofits with business perspective and expertise. In that regard, Maureen became a poster child for the potential of the sabbatical program.

Volunteerism Enhances the Workforce

Research indicates that volunteerism at the workplace is a key driver for positive worker attitudes. One study finds that individuals who participate in employer-sponsored community activities are 30 percent more likely to want to continue working for that company and to help make it a success.[17]

Maureen's volunteer experience confirms the research. "I came back to Timberland after my sabbatical with increased vigor to sell a lot of boots and shirts so that we can continue programs like this," she says. She also reports that her volunteer assignment gave her more confidence to tackle tasks that are not in her job description. At SASS, Maureen was pushed to use skills that she never even knew she possessed. "In the corporate environment, you take on a role and you settle into it," she explains. "But in a new environment, I had new demands placed on me, and it was gratifying to know that I could meet the challenge."

Timberland counts on the fact that the positive energy of enthused volunteers will have a ripple effect across the company. After her return, Maureen had the opportunity to share her sabbatical experience at a companywide gathering. A couple of dozen of her colleagues later approached her to inquire if SASS would be having a special project that needed volunteer support. Others shared that they had a friend who needed help, asking how they could get in touch with SASS.

Just as poor morale can spread like a virus throughout a corporation, zeal can be contagious. Maureen shares that many of her coworkers at Timberland are in their twenties or early thirties and get frustrated by the way the corporate culture works at times. Perhaps a business decision is made that they do not agree with, and they threaten to head out the door. "I tell them that in the long run, one big company operates like another," says Maureen. "But Timberland gives us so many opportunities to develop our skills and contribute to our community; those opportunities are unique in the corporate world."

COMMUNITY INVESTMENT: GENERAL MOTORS

It is inspiring to meet a corporate worker who acts as if only heaven can wait. Colette MacNeil is one of those people.

Colette once worked for Saturn, a wholly owned subsidiary of General Motors, monitoring its Internet communication with customers.[18] In 1999, she applied to join a new unit General Motors was forming called e-GM. It was to be a skunkworks, or experimental, project using the Internet to streamline GM's business operations and enhance the auto manufacturer's consumer relationships worldwide.

When Colette met with e-GM's chief, Mark Hogan, for a first interview, she asked him bluntly, "What could I do that no one else is doing?" Hogan pointed her to a list of work projects scribbled on a white board in his office and said, "You look at this board and tell me."[19]

Two words stood alone on the board without a manager or budget line attached to them: *community* and *household*. Colette asked Hogan why they were there. He explained that he was looking for a way to use technology to advantage the lives of people both inside and outside GM. He admitted that he still had not worked out how to make that happen. Colette asked him if she could take on the challenge.

Making Neighborhoods Positive Places

I met Colette shortly after. Having learned about my uncommon mix of interests in technology, business, and social development, she flew out to California to pick my brain about practical strategies for e-GM. I readily admit that when we first met, I sized her up as a sincere person whose dreams would be crushed by corporate bureaucracy. After all, she was not trying to create a small community project; she wanted to shake up General Motors.

At our first meeting, Colette pulled out of her Franklin organizer a tattered clipping that she had cut out of a newspaper a year before. The article featured Think Detroit, a program dedicated to youth in urban Detroit. The nonprofit sponsors a series of sports leagues and uses that platform to hook the kids into other programs. In its computer skills project, for instance, kids learn how to operate a computer and use the Internet. Once they reach proficiency, they are challenged to teach those skills to their families. After an entire family completes a training program, it receives its own computer.

From the moment Colette ran across the newspaper story, she yearned to be in a position to help Think Detroit. Now she saw her chance. Think Detroit's office is located only three blocks from e-GM's building. That fact alone attracted Hogan to the idea of partnering with the group: "To be a stakeholder in Detroit, we need to do our part to make neighborhoods a positive place to work and live. Adding to our community's intellectual capital was an ideal role for us to play."

E-GM made a $3 million grant over three years to help Think Detroit bring technology to inner-city families. With this financial boost, the nonprofit was able to expand its computer-training program from 172 kids to well over 4,000.

Colette was only getting started. She sensed that there were other people at GM like herself who would be enthused to support community groups but did not know how to help, or perhaps where to begin. So she created WebHands, a matching service for linking her GM colleagues up with soup kitchens, food pantries, and literacy centers. People with skills and resources to share are matched with community organizations with those needs. Most professional workers have an extra suit hanging in the closet that they no longer wear or books that sit on their shelves gathering dust. "Free up what you have and aren't using anyway," is the slogan Colette sent out to them.

Colette promoted WebHands heavily within GM. The corporation also gave it prime real estate on its GM.com Web site, which attracts close to 25 million visitors a month. "My agenda was to hook up people at GM—and subsequently anyone who made contact with our company—back into their communities," she explains. Colette adds that the benefits flow in both directions: "GM workers take their own kids to volunteer in the community, and that gives them something new to talk about at the dinner table."

Colette brings an unorthodox approach to corporate community investment. She does not like to see community groups overly dependent on a single corporate donor because that makes them vulnerable. Once economies tighten, corporations may be forced to cut back their support, and the work of the local organization is put in jeopardy.

For that reason, Colette made sure that WebHands had a self-sustaining revenue model and that e-GM would transfer full ownership of the program over to the community. Web-Hands today is owned jointly by sixteen community organizations, and it is completely autonomous of e-GM.

Innovation Is Contagious

Launching a new initiative may feel like pushing a cart up a hill at first, but help eventually arrives from the most unlikely of places. WebHands was up and running, and its homespun wisdom—"free up what you have but don't use"—had infused the company culture. Then one day Colette received a visit from e-GM's legal counsel. He reported that the General Motors legal team had been ruminating over all the unused patents the company held. Patents are not ideas themselves, but the legal instruments that prevent anyone else from exploiting the ideas they describe. To reach a licensing agreement on a patent is a time-consuming and costly process. For that reason, patents sit idle inside many corporations, incurring costs.

A Harvard University study estimates that over 60 percent of the technology patents held by U.S. companies are never used. European companies do not

Breaking New Ground on Corporate Initiatives in the Community

- Throw out philanthropy models that create dependence.

- Connect individual workers to community groups that need help.

- Leverage the capital of the corporation—technical, intellectual, financial—to help neighborhood networks.

- Pass ownership of programs over to community groups.

use 75 percent of their patents.[20] That's a lot of intellectual capital lying dormant on corporate shelves.

GM's legal team came up with an innovative idea: Why not give the patents away? That would get expensive intellectual properties off the books and cut the firm's legal costs. They asked Colette and her colleagues at Think Detroit to figure out a solution for delivering patents to universities and other public groups that could make good use of the research. Months later, PatentDonors.com emerged from the e-GM tech lab.

Here's how it works: A corporation pays a $2,750 fee to list a patent on the Web site. Universities and other public research centers can sign up for free memberships enabling them to search for patents that might be useful for their own research. A corporation can anonymously donate its patents for a donation tax credit of around 35 percent of the value of the patent. Chalk up a substantial corporate gain on its investment. The recipient university also scores a big win, acquiring a potentially valuable patent at no cost.

And there's more. The benefits also go back to grassroots community groups. When a university chooses a patent, the donor corporation pays an additional fee of 1.5 to 2.5 percent of the patent's value. These fees go to Think Detroit to fund its technology transfer program with low-income urban families. Colette estimates that values range from about $5 million for a single patent to $15 million for a cluster of patents that are useless alone. That's not exactly chump change going back to the community. Consistent with its principles, e-GM once again gave ownership of the site and all intellectual property associated with it over to Think Detroit.

When some of the world's best ideas, held captive in unused patents, start being freed up to energize new entrepreneurial activity, that's a big win for the general economy as well.

COMMUNITY AT THE CORE: HANNA ANDERRSON

Most parents could recognize Hanna Anderrson clothes even if the company's name is unfamiliar to them. At the local playground or at preschool, they may have taken note of the bright colors and comfy design that characterize Hanna's look. It's kid-cool in a way that leopard tights and leather jackets on young children never can be.

Hanna sends out over 14 million catalogues a year targeted to a relatively high-income demographic.[21] Yet you may see a child sporting its gear at a homeless shelter as easily as you would in an upscale neighborhood. If that sounds like a riddle, think hand-me-downs.

Back in 1983, Gun Denhart was frustrated by her inability to find soft 100 percent cotton clothing for her three-year-old son. So she and her husband, Tom, a New York advertising executive, threw caution to the wind, migrated across the country, and launched a children's clothing company out of their new home in Portland, Oregon. They named the company in honor of Gun's grandmother, Hanna Anderrson.

The couple produced their first product catalogue at the kitchen table, laboriously gluing one-inch-square swatches of fabric onto seventy-five thousand catalogues. Before long, thousands of boxes of clothes and twenty workers filled every nook and cranny in their home; at one point, even the sauna was filled with turtlenecks.

Before long, it came time to put out another catalogue. On this second effort, the Denharts wanted to brand the durability and quality of Hanna's product line. They hit on a message they liked: "Your kids will outgrow the clothes before the clothes wear out." To support that message, the couple devised a creative marketing program based on the concept of hand-me-downs. Customers were invited to send used Hannawear back to the company and in return receive a 20 percent discount off their next purchase. The Hannadowns program was born.

Gun readily admits that she never made a plan as to how to handle the second-hand clothes. She had to do something with the growing pile, however, so she donated them to nonprofit groups aiding children in the Portland area.

That was her introduction to the needs of poor children in America. Gun was born and raised in Sweden and came to the United States as a young adult. "It was an unbelievable eye-opener for me; I didn't know that people could be so poor in this country," she says. Gun also was deeply moved by the letters of thanks she received from parents who were receiving Hannadowns at a homeless center or a women's shelter.

Gun resolved to do more. She created channels to distribute clothes to kids' programs across America. Gun estimates the company has given out well over 1 million articles of high-quality clothing to needy children over the years. Although only a small portion of Hanna customers ever actually participated in the Hannadowns program, nearly every customer came to identify the company with the values that the program represented.

In 1990, Gun bumped into the Social Venture Network (SVN), a gathering of entrepreneurs who aim to do well in business by promoting the social good. Some of the early founders of SVN included Ben Cohen of Ben & Jerry's Ice Cream fame and Anita Roddick of the Body Shop. The SVN promotes the idea that a business is at its best when it pursues a triple bottom line: financial profitability, benefits for people and communities, and environmental sustainability.

Until that time, Hanna had made donations to community groups out of its corporate profits in a haphazard way. Inspired by the other SVN members, Gun adopted a more structured donor program. The company began sharing 5 percent of its pretax profit annually to support needy children. It directs most of those funds to children's projects in the communities where the company does business. In addition to its corporate headquarters in Portland, Hanna operates ten retail outlets across the United States. Workers at each location help to choose which community groups to support.

Despite her company's remarkable generosity, Gun does not want anyone to turn her into a saint. "I really mean it when I say that my decisions have been strictly about business, always," she declares. Gun realizes that her claim may sound

---

The Branding of Hanna Anderrson: Community at the Core

- Link consumer activity to tangible community benefits.

- Build an emotional bridge connecting young parents and children in need.

- Provide strong family benefits to the company's own employees.

- Gift 5 percent of pretax profits to children's groups.

- Involve employees in the choice and development of community partnerships.

- Set up a brand-associated foundation to advocate for children's empowerment.

strange, so she quickly adds, "You can't run a healthy company in an unhealthy community; if the community falls apart, your company will suffer as well."

Community Values Inside and Outside the Company

Gun's knack for using her own felt needs to build a bridge—she had trouble finding comfortable and attractive clothes for her own child, so other parents must have the same need—is the real genius behind Hanna's success. She brought that empathy to running the company as well. She treated her workers as she herself would like to be treated. The genesis of the company's child care policy is a good example. Gun had a brood of six children when she launched Hanna. Until she found secure child care, she found it hard to stay focused on her work. That struggle led her to take note of other women who worked for the company. "I was drawn especially to one woman who was divorced and had two little kids at home, and we were paying her five dollars an hour," she recalls. "I knew what child care cost, so I asked myself, 'How could she make this work?'"

At a time when few companies were reaching out to working families, Hanna Anderrson introduced a policy to pay 50 percent of its workers' child care expenses. The company also became a pioneer in offering flex-time. "As the world changes and you don't have family nearby, your company becomes a part of your life," Gun says, explaining the philosophy behind Hanna's employee benefits. "How people feel while they're at work becomes incredibly important."

In the catalogue business, call centers particularly have trouble attracting qualified personnel and suffer from high turnover rates. Not so at Hanna. A combination of humane work policies and a mission that stands for something makes a big difference for its workers.

Just ask Joan Ritchie. Before she came to Hanna, Joan worked at a major department store in the Portland area.[22] After ten years of service, she took time off to deliver and nurture her first child. When she returned to work, the department store downgraded her work evaluations. "I was sure it reflected the fact that my boss did not think women with children should be working," Joan says.

Her family and friends encouraged her to apply at Hanna. "It has a reputation in the Portland area of being friendly to working mothers," reports Joan. Despite her management background in retail, Joan went after a clerk position at a Hannah outlet store to get her foot in the door. Thirteen years and several promotions later, she still works at Hanna.

What has kept Joan at Hanna for so many years? Joan points to the promotion of community values both inside and outside the company. She feels inspired working for a company that so closely ties its corporate values to helping children in need and that's mirrored in the way the company treats her family. Joan says she's not alone: "Once employees start working here, nobody wants to leave."

A Loyal Following Translates into Market Value

Gun and her investors sold Hanna to Dorset Capital, a private investment group, in 2001. She remains on the board of directors in a nonexecutive role. The Denharts wanted to spend more time with their own grandchildren and pursue other personal interests. At the top of that list is the newly formed Hanna Anderrson Children's Foundation, which Gun is heading up.

The foundation leverages Hanna's brand name to support community programs in addressing children's health and education. The foundation also lobbies on the legislative level to make children's issues a top priority in how public money is spent.

Dorset Capital has decided to continue directing 5 percent of the company's profits to benefit children. "It's a sizeable chunk of money, but we see it as a worthwhile investment in community building and valuable branding," says Jeff Mills, a Dorset Capital partner.[23] Mills believes that Hanna is distinct in the kids' clothing market precisely because it marries profitability and good community principles. When his investment group carried out due diligence on the company, it found an incredibly high loyalty among both customers and employees. "If it looked like just any other kids' clothing retailer out there, Hanna probably would lose its customer base and many of its employees," says Mills. "This company's road to success has been paved with a human touch."

Marking the Return on Community Engagement

The models of engagement featured in this chapter give a sense of the range of relationships a firm can build with local communities. It's intriguing to note not only the diversity in the means but also in the objectives. Timberland is fully transparent that its foremost goal in promoting employee volunteering is the development of its own people. Ahold invests in the community to stimulate new markets for its products. e-GM pours resources into its community so that it will be a healthier place to live and work.

It's important to establish from the start the prime objectives of community engagement. If a firm does not know its destination, then just about any road will get it there. Oddly enough, lots of different stakeholders will then ascribe an agenda to the project that may or may not match the firm's intention. But a clearly defined destination will set the appropriate expectations both inside and outside the firm.

For most senior managers, this first query—Why are we doing this?—is surpassed in importance by a second query—What are we getting out of this? For that reason, every project that hopes to be sustainable into the future will need to calculate a return on community engagement (RCE).

Three specific areas of RCE are worthwhile tracking: (1) the tangible benefits of community-based programs on local residents, such as jobs created and the number of people touched; (2) the direct business benefits that result from community-based programs, such as new customers gained and employees recruited and retained; and (3) the correlation between invested resources and targeted goals.

A Boston College study of 222 community relations managers from U.S. corporations indicates that RCE evaluation is sorely lacking in the corporate world. Only 36 percent of the managers report that their companies have developed a system

Return on Community Engagement Measures . . .

○ The direct benefit to community stakeholders

○ The direct benefit to business operations

○ The correlation between invested resources and targeted goals to account for the resources they provide to the community (for example, grants, in-kind donations, employee time) across all departments and sites. A mere 14 percent of the managers have a process to evaluate and measure the internal impact of their community programs, and only 12 percent evaluate the total impact of corporate engagement on the community.[24]

There's lots of room for improvement here, but it's not a matter of incompetence. The results of the study more likely point to a lack of priority. You can tell what's most valuable to a firm by looking at what gets measured. Senior managers understandably are more preoccupied by metrics of winning and keeping customers.

In the next chapter, on customer care, we will see that the continuum from community engagement to customer relationship is much shorter than some managers imagine.

Chapter Four

Customer Care

Principle Four

A company will represent its products honestly
to customers and honor their dignity up to
and beyond a transaction.

Vital Signs

Is customer service a company priority? Does the company
take responsibility when any of its products becomes a public
hazard? Does the company design with the health and safety
of its consumers in mind? Is the company honest in its communication with customers? Does the company give fair representation of its products and services? Does the company act
in good faith throughout the transaction process? Does the
company make promises that it cannot meet? Are the privacy
rights of consumers respected? Are mistakes quickly admitted
and rectified? Are the price points for goods and services
transparent? Is product research reported accurately? Do sales

channels rely on conflicts of interest? Are the people closest to the customer empowered to make decisions?

The formula for doing well at business looks quite simple on paper: provide goods and services that are superior in quality, sell them at a reasonable cost, and meet customers' needs beyond the transaction.

Commerce rarely plays out like this in the rough-and-tumble market economy, of course. Customers struggle to differentiate among product offerings, and price points are rarely straightforward. Companies fill the perception gap with marketing campaigns that can obscure as much as they clarify.

The cellular phone industry exemplifies the obscure. The average consumer despairs when it comes to choosing among providers. Few can make heads or tails of that maze referred to as a calling plan.

The disconnect takes place at the level of expectation. For customers, a telephone call is nothing more than that: a call. Cellular companies are trying to sell relationships, however, not telephone calls. In fact, customer relationships are nurtured, not manufactured, and so it is ill advised for any company to treat a relationship as a commodity. It is no wonder that customer loyalty has proven to be a real stumbling block for cellular providers.

When customers start running the other way, some companies may turn desperate. In the summer of 2002, telecom regulators in California opened an investigation into Cingular Wireless, America's second largest cellular carrier. The regulatory agency accused Cingular of acting "fundamentally unfair to consumers" by locking them into long-term contracts and then failing to provide promised services. When customers tried to cancel their subscriptions, Cingular allegedly threatened to slap them with a termination fee of $150 or more.[1]

Trying to force consumers into loyalty rarely works. Customers need a reason to believe in what a company does. They may respond to seeing an ad or using a product or talking with a company agent. Each point of contact cements or, alternatively, undermines their emotional attachment to the company. Their loyalty grows only after their basic demands for trust, security, usefulness, and fair exchange are met.

A recent telephone exchange I had with a sales agent illustrates the relationship disconnect well. The agent, who claimed to represent AT&T Wireless, reached me at my home and made an attractive offer: I would receive a free cellular phone and a trove of minutes at no cost for the first six months of a one-year contract.

I thought that this plan might be a good start for my oldest daughter, who is just entering junior high. As soon as I expressed my interest, the agent asked for my credit card data and social security number.

At that point, my suspicion kicked in. How did I know for sure this guy actually did represent AT&T

**Customer Loyalty:
You Know It Don't Come Easy**

CEOs name their top four management challenges:

- Customer loyalty and retention (37 percent)

- Increasing flexibility and speed (34 percent)

- Managing mergers and acquisitions (33 percent)

- Downward pressure on prices (33 percent)

Source: The CEO Challenge: Top Marketplace and Management Issues 2001 (New York: Conference Board/Accenture, 2001).

Wireless? Couldn't anyone pull a number out of the phone book, make a bogus yet compelling offer, and walk away with my vital personal data? I told the agent I would be happy to accept his offer as long as I could call him back at what I could be assured to be an AT&T Wireless contact number. He told me he could not do that, so I asked to speak with his supervisor.

The supervisor came on the line, and I explained to him my concern. I reiterated my willingness to call back and engage his firm in a service contract. He too declined that request. Then out of frustration with me, he made a remarkable retort: "Listen, you just have to trust us. We are demonstrating our trust in you by offering you a free phone. It's only fair that you trust us enough to believe we really are who we say we are."

I did not enter into a contract with AT&T Wireless that day. In order for trust to extend both ways in a business relationship, basic conditions have to be met. If the risk is high and the security is low, customers are likely to turn away. Cellular companies these days are hearing plenty of customer complaints about dropped connections. I wonder if they realize the problem extends well beyond technology?

The corporate world has fallen into a crisis of customer care. Indeed, the failure to practice fair exchange is the most telling sign of a corporation that has lost its soul. Whenever I meet with senior managers of a company, I ask them four quick questions, and their answers tell me a great deal about how well their firm takes care of the customer. Try it out, and see how a company that you are close to stacks up:

- What overt promises does the company make to customers, and do those promises truly identify what it can deliver?

- Do the firm's operations, from marketing to sales to fulfillment, respect the dignity of customers?
- When the company fails a customer, how fast does it move to make amends?
- Does the company make meaningful changes in response to customer needs and feedback?

Let's take a look at the thorniest obstacles to building customer relationships on a solid foundation of trust and consider a number of actions to overcome them.

KICKING BAD HABITS

Zachary Bentley says he's no Ralph Nader. The business manager and corporate officer of a drug infusion service, Ven-A-Care, based in Key West, Florida, is shaking up the pharmaceutical industry all the same.[2]

Zachary never planned to lead a crusade for corporate reform. In 1990, he simply was sitting at his desk wading through paperwork, when he noticed something amiss with a Medicare payment. He received a fifty-six-dollar reimbursement for a pharmaceutical that had cost his company only ten dollars. In theory, 80 percent of the drug was to be paid for by Medicare and 20 percent by the beneficiary. Zachary did some quick math and figured that the beneficiary's copayment alone surpassed the actual cost of the drug. Convinced that the Florida Medicare carrier had erred, he tore up the check and asked the agency to reprocess the reimbursement. Days later, the carrier got back to him and informed him that there had been no mistake.

Puzzled, Zachary searched for answers. What he found shocked him. More than a few doctors and clinics are billing

Medicare based on wholesale prices that pharmaceutical companies give the government program. The pharmaceutical companies then sell the drugs to the health care providers at a much lower cost. The providers reap exorbitant profits and, because the windfall operates like a government-funded kickback, pharmaceutical companies also come out big winners.[3]

Zachary reported his discovery to federal and state agencies and was troubled by their muted response. He knew intimately the impact of skyrocketing drug costs on people suffering from debilitating illness. At the time, Ven-A-Care primarily delivered intravenous drug care to clients in their homes as an alternative to visiting a hospital. Most of its business was AIDS related, and Ven-A-Care gained local acclaim for extending treatment to patients even after their health insurance ran out.

In an ironic twist of fate, the kickback program would threaten the survival of Ven-A-Care a year later. It all started when National Medical Care, a leading kidney dialysis chain then owned by W. R. Grace & Co., invited Ven-A-Care to join in a new business venture in 1991. The proposal included doctors who were in a position to prescribe expensive infusion drugs to AIDS patients. "They promised us that we would become wealthy if we shared drug revenues with the physicians because they would order large amounts of drugs that cost far less than the prices reported to Medicare," recalls Zachary. The scheme had already had paid off handsomely for National Medical Care in the kidney dialysis business, he alleges, and the company saw an opportunity to expand the model to AIDS treatment.

When Zachary and his partners declined to join the venture, National Medical Care instead enticed several Key West physicians who up to that time had referred their clients almost exclusively to Ven-A-Care to order drugs directly through its system. In several cases, National Medical Care employees went into the doctors' offices and started handling their billing practice. Ven-A-Care's business took a serious hit; the owners cut salaries and took out loans to keep the company afloat.

Zachary was furious. "We had worked hard to build a reputable business that provided a quality service at reasonable prices," he says. "To be wiped out when you're trying to do the right thing is a bitter pill to swallow."

Zachary hit back hard: he and his partners filed a civil suit charging National Medical Care for using fraudulent practices to steal their business. Although they eventually settled the suit for undisclosed terms, documents unearthed during litigation revealed that National Medical Care's pricing practices had defrauded government health programs and patients out of hundreds of millions of dollars. "You could say they wrote the book on corporate corruption; practically every fraud you could commit against Medicare they were doing," reports Zachary.

The federal False Claims Act permits individual companies to file lawsuits on behalf of the government to expose corporate fraud. In 1994, Ven-A-Care filed a federal suit accusing National Medical Care of scamming Medicare and Medicaid at its kidney dialysis clinics. The U.S. Justice Department deemed the allegations so significant it took over the case. Six years later, the government settled, and National Medical Care (which had since been acquired by Fresenius Medical Care of Lexington, Massachusetts) was forced to pay back $486 million.

When monetary damages result from a federal false claims suit, the whistle-blower is entitled to a slice of the funds. Therefore, the government subsequently awarded Ven-A-Care $40 million. Given the amount of money involved, it's fair to ask whether Zachary and his partners had become glorified gold diggers. "The accusation would not surprise me," says Zachary with characteristic candor. "We have profited very well from our activity, but we also have saved the government a tremendous amount of money."

While pursuing litigation, Zachary and his partners made a valiant effort to rebuild their business, shifting Ven-A-Care's business to the delivery of oncology drug therapies. But the company ran into a familiar kickback scheme, this time with oncologists.

Making a Killing on Health Care

These numbers reveal prices for several drugs offered by major drug makers since 1997:

Drug and Maker	Medicare Pays Doctor	Actual Price Doctors Pay	Profit
Vancomycin, Abbott Labs	$261.84	$76.00	$185.84
Etopside, Gensia	134.87	14.00	120.87
Bleomycin, Pharmacia-Upjohn	294.48	154.85	139.63
Vincasar, Pharmacia-Upjohn	704.43	7.50	696.93

Source: J. Appleby, "Drugmakers Accused of 'Unethical' Pricing," *USA Today*, Sept. 27, 2000.

"Profit maximization—it's in the bag," promises a marketing memo that Ven-A-Care received from one major drug maker. The Glaxo Wellcome marketing document details how an oncology practice using its antinausea drug treatment could net millions of dollars more than if it used a competitor's product due to its discounted price below "wholesale" (read: the price it sets to Medicare for the drug).[4]

Convinced that it could not operate with integrity in its drug infusion practice, Ven-A-Care turned into a full-time whistle-blower. "We were fed up, and decided to shine the light of day on these shady practices," says Zachary. His company has since been party to several lawsuits against major drug companies, including a fraudulent pricing case the U.S. government successfully settled with Bayer in 2000.[5]

Pharmaceutical companies live a strange contradiction. Just about all Americans could spin a warm tale about how a drug has made a huge difference in the life of someone they hold dear. But turn the conversation toward pharmaceutical companies, and you best stand back and duck lest you get torched by the rage.

It would be presumptuous to offer in a handful of paragraphs a magic elixir for what ails the pharmaceutical industry. But if drug makers truly want to clean up their act, they have to give people less cause to find fault. Following is a short prescription to start the healing process (when applying to other industries, adjust the dosage as needed). All of the remedies mirror one common theme: honor the dignity of the customer. If a corporation would adopt that single goal and evaluate every aspect of its business operation from that standard, customer retention would cease to be a problem.

Rx One: Don't Hide Your Price Under a Bushel

Rising health care costs in the United States have stabilized in the past few years with one exception: the price of prescription drugs. Zachary Bentley clarifies that he is not fighting the escalating cost of drugs. He has a much more modest goal: to demand that drug companies practice transparency in pricing. Once fair representation is achieved, he argues, government and health insurance groups can make informed decisions about what they can afford to pay.

Zachary points to the state of Missouri where funding for school transportation and special education had to be cut, a decision that state officials directly attribute to rising Medicaid drug costs. "The health insurance system is going to be like a dog chasing its tail until there's some transparency in pricing. When you have seniors out there eating dog food because they can't afford the price of their drugs, that's a sad state of affairs."

Rx Two: Disclose Fully What a Product Can and Cannot Do

Television ads for prescription drugs, which were all but outlawed as recently as five years ago, are now taking over television airtime. Pharmaceutical companies spent an estimated $1.8 billion on television advertising in 2001, 50 percent more than what they spent in 1999.[6] The United States is now one of only two countries in the world where prescriptions are hawked in prime time.

The Federal Drug Administration (FDA) sends out over a hundred letters a year to pharmaceutical companies demanding changes in television commercials, magazine ads, and other promotional materials. Several companies are repeat offenders. The FDA chastised Pfizer/Pharmacia, for example, three times for airing grossly misleading television ads that promote its arthritis drug, Celebrex. Pfizer's ad shows people with arthritis performing such strenuous activities as rowing a boat and riding a scooter. To put it mildly, the ad overstated the benefit of its product for individuals with chronic arthritis.[7]

Classical free market economists tell us that people make rational, free choices based on their self-interest and complete information. Commercial practices are rarely that respectable. Much of advertising seeks to entice and shame the buying public into a sale. Consumer ads can be an important tool to educate the public about advances in drug therapy and may even encourage people to seek out help for untreated maladies. But ads also can deceive people to pursue drugs that will not help them, and may even do them harm.

At a minimum, drug makers ought to continue to disclose the risks and side effects of medication they promote in their advertising. Some pharmaceutical companies are pressuring the FDA to change that rule, but the effort is misguided.[8] Drug makers should be guided by the age-old principle for the delivery of medical care: "First, do no harm."

Rx Three: Bridge the Credibility Gap in Industry Research

Drug makers are giving medical research a bad name; perhaps only the tobacco industry has so profoundly undermined the veracity of scientific studies. In several high-profile cases, senior doctors accepted large sums of money from drug companies to sign articles that they did not even write endorsing new medicines.[9]

Such egregious violations should not blunt the more subtle misrepresentations that plague the industry. The *Journal of the American Medical Association* (JAMA) published in 2002 a highly critical overview of the way drug trials are done and reported, asserting that drug makers regularly massage their data to make new treatments appear better than they actually are.[10]

If pharmaceutical companies plan to continue to sponsor medical research—though a movement toward independent research may be the sole path to restore confidence in drug studies—scientists must be given license to publish complete and even contradictory results.

Rx Four: Don't Build Your Sales Channels on Conflicts of Interest

Ven-A-Care discovered that a fair number of doctors and other care providers are willing to select drugs for their patients based on the reimbursements they can receive from health insurance. The news gets worse. Some physicians, in exchange for money, are allowing pharmaceutical sales representatives into their examining rooms to meet with patients, review medical charts, and even recommend which medicines to prescribe. In a survey of doctors in Maryland, 37 percent admit they accept some kind of compensation from pharmaceutical companies.[11]

Rx: Two Final, and Radical, Proposals

Because the implications of these practices for public health are so frightening, my final two proposals are a bit more radical.

First, it is time to call these "marketing inducements" what they truly are, kickback bribes, and prosecute doctors and drug makers on that basis. Second, pharmaceutical companies ought seriously to reevaluate how much money they spend on marketing relative to research and development. Making promises becomes a heck of a lot easier when you have high-quality products that can deliver.

Does Your Customer Have a Face?

Under new legislation signed into law by President Bill Clinton in 1999, banks, brokerage houses, and insurance companies were freed up to combine under the same roof. Financial institutions immediately searched for merger opportunities, salivating at the chance to mine each other's customer lists and pitch a full line of related products and services.

So financial institutions get the chance to become more profitable. What's in it for you and me, other than more junk mail and telemarketing calls? At this early stage, it seems the answer is, Not much.

Financial institutions can hand out personal information from your bank account, brokerage account, or insurance records to all its divisions and affiliates. They also can share your private data with outside telemarketers, with whom they have written joint selling agreements. We don't have the right to take our names off these marketing lists.

As a journalist, I investigated how banks, which traditionally guarded their customers' privacy with the utmost care, now liberally use their customer data to market new services. Data-mining software makes it increasingly simple for private information to be gathered, correlated, and retrieved. What companies do with that information in the name of marketing can be troubling.[12] Consider this fictional scenario:

The Springers, a family of four, hold a range of financial service accounts at the First Wholly United Bank. A review of Ms. Springer's latest credit card purchases suggests that she may be expecting a new child; she has been making quite a few purchases at baby clothing shops and even made a payment to a diaper delivery service. It looks like a good moment for First Wholly United Bank's insurance affiliate to make a sales call to the Springer household and ask whether they would like to augment their life insurance policy to secure the future for any dependents they might one day leave behind.

Several months later, the bank's data retrieval system sends an alert that Mr. Springer's employer has ceased to make a direct deposit into the family savings account over several consecutive paychecks. A red flag is attached to the Springers' account. Sure enough, a week later, Mr. Springer calls in to ask for an extension on his account credit line. The customer service agent notes the flag and informs Mr. Springer that an extension on his credit line will not be available at this time. He is encouraged to try again in several months; the system will continue to monitor the direct deposits, of course.

First Wholly United Bank attaches three ratings to the personal portfolio of every one of its customers: a credit risk score, the return on investment (ROI) a customer contributes to the bank across his or her various accounts with the bank, and what is referred to in-house as the PIN (or pain-in-the-neck) rating, given to customers who eat up large chunks of employee time with their account questions.

Fortunately for Mr. Springer, despite his apparent layoff from work, he's a low credit risk and has a high ROI and a low

PIN rating. When he calls in to the customer service center to see if he can refinance his mortgage, his telephone number is identified, and his favorable overall rating puts him directly through to a customer care representative.

Several minutes later, Mr. Springer's neighbor, Mr. Batstone, calls the bank. His ROI is quite low and his PIN rating is unreasonably high; his customer service call is identified, and he is put on hold. After thirty minutes on hold, Mr. Batstone gets frustrated and hangs up the telephone. It's not a loss for the bank; after all, he had a low ROI and a high PIN.

Perhaps my scenario is a bit exaggerated, but not nearly as much you might think. The technical capability and access to data are already in place at most major corporations. The sensitivity to consumer privacy remains the highest hurdle to implementing bold marketing initiatives.

Companies are right to tread lightly. Merchants that trade on privacy are walking on thin ice. A deep consumer backlash is brewing.

There's a second marketing issue implicit in the banking scenario, and it's tinted with even more shades of gray. The retrieval and evaluation of data allow for a sophisticated profiling of each individual customer, which makes a tiered delivery of customer service a possibility.

A senior executive of a major credit card company in fact shared with me that his company moved to a rendition of this stealth strategy. An internal analysis of the ROI of each of the firm's customers indicated that 10 to 15 percent of its clients were providing 90 percent of its profit margin. From that moment forward, the credit card firm determined to devote its customer care to that elite slice of its customer base and give only the most minimal possible care to the low ROI set.

It only makes sense that a firm would want to take extra good care of its best customers; their loyalty to the company is an important asset. But at the same time, it's foolish to treat customer care as if it were a scarce commodity. There's no reason to ignore the face of any customer. As the following case of the ServiceMaster Company shows, the decline of customer care is usually not traced to the scarcity of time but the overabundance of bureaucracy in the organization.

EMPOWERING WORKERS
CLOSEST TO THE CUSTOMER

Is it possible to control the quality of the customer experience at a large corporation? A small business works hard to satisfy expectations because it cannot afford to lose a single customer. Most of us assume that after the company reaches a certain size, it loses its capacity to deliver personal care. Not Bill Pollard, the former CEO and chairman of the ServiceMaster Company, which offers a wide range of commercial and residential services: home and office cleaning, lawn care, termite and pest control, plumbing, and furniture maintenance. "My goal is to bring the spirit of a small company and its responsiveness to customer needs into a big organization," he declares.[13]

Bill has confronted the challenges of major growth, having steered a modest firm into a Fortune 500 corporation. When he arrived at ServiceMaster in 1977, the company had annual sales of $200 million; those figures had soared to over $6 billion by the time he resigned as chairman of the board in early 2002.

Even when ServiceMaster was a much smaller enterprise, ensuring a high quality of customer care was not easy, shares

Bill. The biggest obstacle is that its workforce does not operate under one roof. Most of its employees work at the customer site, which means there is no direct line of management supervising them when they are delivering service.

ServiceMaster has developed a series of tools to surmount this obstacle. The most important innovation, at least at a structural level, was the application of an industrial engineering model to service delivery. It is hard to imagine how a subjective practice like satisfying customer expectations could be so quantified, but Bill's team broke down the delivery of service into five-minute components, starting from the moment a customer makes an order and ending when the bill is paid. "We carefully looked at that continuum to determine whether an individual increment was producing a meaningful benefit for the customer, or alternatively was a wasted effort," Bill explains.

A highly regimented system runs the risk of making the people who deliver the service feel as if they are widgets at the end of the corporate chain. "To make the system idiot-proof can make them feel like an idiot," Bill says more bluntly.

To provide some needed balance, everyone in ServiceMaster during Bill's leadership was asked at least once a year to work a full shift of front-line service. Managers thereby gain a personal understanding of what service workers do on the job, how they feel about their tasks, and the customer expectations they meet along the way. Over his career, Bill himself spent at least three days a year on the front lines and claims that he learned something new each time about what the company was imposing on service workers.

When worker performance declines, managers all too often jump to the conclusion that their employees are lazy or unskilled. Bill takes a different route: he starts with the assumption that the

Bringing the Spirit of a Small Business into a Large Corporation

ServiceMaster has discovered six key elements:

1. Break down and evaluate discrete components of your customer service.

2. Periodically place every person in the company in a position to have direct contact with customer service.

3. Push decision making to the people who are closest to the customer.

4. Flatten the organization; slim down an expanding midriff.

5. Keep customer acquisition close to the point of delivery.

6. Reward employees for successful levels of customer acquisition and retention.

service worker wants to perform to the best of his or her ability. "It's more likely that we are laying a bag of rocks on their back in the way we're asking them to do their job," he asserts.

A day of manual labor also helps to instill company leaders with humility. Bill can attest to that. Not long after he arrived at ServiceMaster, he joined up with the housekeeping team at a hospital to spend the day cleaning hallways, patient rooms, and bathrooms.

As he was pushing a mop and bucket along a hospital corridor, a woman stopped and asked him, "Aren't you Bill Pollard?" Once he confirmed his identity, the woman introduced herself as a distant relative of his wife. She then took full note of Bill and his mop, cocked her head, and asked, "Aren't you a lawyer?" Bill replied that he indeed once practiced law, but had recently taken a new job. Taking account of the busy flow of people moving up and down the corridor, the woman turned red and leaned toward Bill, whispering, "Is everything all right at home?"

The higher up the ladder one moves in a corporation, the less that individual may know about what the customer really wants and needs. Because Bill firmly believes that maxim, he aims to push decision making to the people who are closest to the customer. A company operates at its peak when workers are empowered to make decisions and are measured by results. Take away that right, and responsibility and customer care will suffer.

A recent experience I had with my water utility company suggests how far off this mark a company can fall. When a water main burst on the street in front of my driveway, the gushing water poured down an incline and into my garage. I made an urgent call to the water company hot line, and within hours a local contractor came out to my home. But it was a Saturday afternoon, and the contractor informed me that unfortunately, he could not help me until Monday. When I complained that my house might float away by then, he agreed to build a rudimentary dam that would divert the rushing water away from my house and down the street. The water continued to pour out all weekend. On Monday morning, a crew came back out to my house and repaired the water main.

A month later, I received my water bill and was shocked at the amount I was being charged for water usage. It did not take me long to figure out the cause: I was being charged for the water that had poured out of the broken pipe. I called customer service and explained the problem with my bill. The agent checked my account, verified the repair problem, and agreed with my analysis. I was relieved; it looked as if I could put the matter behind me. Then the agent shattered my relief: "I'm sorry I can't do anything about your bill. I can't make billing decisions. I'll have to send a note to the billing department. You can call them in seven to ten days and see what decision they've reached."

The agent did at least assure me that I would not have to pay my bill for another month; she would put a hold on my account, noting possible overcharges. A week or two later, I went through the entire process again with the billing department, which agreed to adjust the overcharges. I suppose I should not have been surprised when the local contractor for the water company came by a couple of weeks later to shut down my water service for having failed to pay my water bill. "A hold on your account? I don't know anything about that," he replied apologetically.

People are imperfect and make mistakes. Customers seem to understand that fact and do not expect perfection as much as they do satisfaction. Contrary to popular belief, a company does not score big points with customers when it calls two weeks later with the message, "Sorry, we messed up, so we'll give you your money back." Customers are more inspired by workers who show responsibility and are willing to make decisions to resolve a problem.

A Harvard study featuring ServiceMaster confirms that dynamic. The study found that more than 50 percent of the time when customers make reference to excellent customer care, they cite an incident when a service provider goofed yet corrected the error on the spot.[14]

To encourage that kind of vitality at ServiceMaster, Bill found that he constantly had to battle bureaucracy and an expanding midriff of middle management. A large corporation by its nature adds layers. Bill argues that the more layers a company has (and here he tips his hat to Peter Drucker), the more noise is generated that distracts workers and drowns out the customer voice. "We constantly struggle to find a better way to flatten our firm," he admits.

Bill also strives to shorten the distance between sales and operations. ServiceMaster has long had a bias to keep customer acquisition close to where the delivery of the service takes place. A good example is how it handles its telemarketing teams. Most of its five hundred branch organizations across the United States deploy an in-house telemarketing system. The company could have farmed out this operation to an outside vendor or centralized its call centers into a few national hubs. Any clever accountant could demonstrate the big cost savings of following either one of these paths.

But focusing on partial financial figures can sometimes lead a company down the wrong path. When Bill's management team did a total cost analysis of its customer acquisition and retention, they discovered that keeping the call centers decentralized at local branch offices was a far more effective and cost-efficient strategy.

The reason can be summed up in one word: accountability. When branch managers arrive at the office each morning, they know immediately whether the previous evening their call center reached its quota for new customer acquisitions. If quotas are not reached, the burden for figuring out why falls squarely on the manager's shoulders. Imagine the alternative: how easy it would be to blame poor performance on an anonymous call center. At ServiceMaster, the same branch office that brings in the customer also delivers the service and follows up on the relationship. It all takes place in one location close to the customer.

When a large enterprise keeps accountability close to the point of delivery, its size becomes less of an obstacle. "Build trust with your customers, respond to their evolving needs, and empower your people to make mistakes when they occur," says Bill. "Do these three things, and you will create an environment for long-lasting customer relationships to grow."

Customers Will Forgive

Companies are not foolproof. At some point, they inevitably fall off the rails. The process of getting back on track is usually quite painful and tests the fiber of the enterprise. As the ServiceMaster experience suggests, customers are willing to forgive mistakes if the problem is confronted openly and with an authentic desire to resolve the difficulty. The worst tack a firm can take is to ignore or cover up instances of product failure or operational error. Untreated, the tumor will spread silently but fatally.

The Odwalla juice company today is a highly successful subsidiary of Coca-Cola. It is a miracle that the company is still in business today, let alone the healthy juice alternative for one of the largest distributors on the globe, because in late 1996, while still an independent company, it faced a crisis that threatened to ruin the company.[15] Health officials linked its apple juice product to an outbreak of *Escherichia coli* bacterial poisoning in Washington State. Most of the victims were children. Odwalla immediately issued a nationwide recall of all its products containing apple juice—thirteen types of juice in all. It would be hard to imagine a worse scenario for a company that built its reputation on wholesome refreshment.

Companies typically don't face the music of public accountability until a crisis strikes. For that reason, the crisis often throws a firm into damage-control mode. Suddenly, workers feel the weight of making decisions that will affect many lives.

Odwalla had wisely had prepared for the storm. Greg Steltenpohl, an Odwalla founder and the chairman during its *E. coli* crisis, relates that when the company was starting off in the early 1980s, it was easy to keep everyone focused. Odwalla's slogan was "juice for humans," and the community atmosphere of a small company reinforced the message.

By 1993, Odwalla had grown significantly, and Greg sensed that it was time for a re-visioning process. "It hit me that only the original core team really understood what we were about," says Greg. "I learned that a corporation needs to refresh its vision and values every ten years."

So Greg and his executive team launched a program that they dubbed Vision Link. Every employee took part in shaping a company credo—what Odwalla wanted to accomplish and how the company would go about doing it. Key vendors and distributors also were part of the discussion. "Too often companies define themselves in a vacuum, as if their customers and suppliers are waiting to be told what the company stands for," says Greg.

The companywide exercise lasted over four months. In the end, the Odwalla workforce determined that they wanted to stand for "ecological leadership and sustainability" in the refreshment market and act with "honesty, integrity, and respect" in their relationships with suppliers, vendors, and customers.

So what's next, we ask cynically: printing out an ethics statement and filing it under the letter "E"?

Once the *E. coli* disaster hit, Odwalla's core values were truly tested. The company set up a crisis center and on its walls prominently posted a copy of the company credo. Several of Odwalla's senior managers reported to me that the core values became a touchstone to how they should act. When complex issues arose, someone would turn to the statement on the wall and say, "Well, if this is who we are, then we have to . . ."

The company immediately recalled its drinks and offered to cover the medical costs of anyone affected by an Odwalla product. Dismissing the counsel of lawyers fearing culpability and lawsuits, Greg and other senior executives personally visited the victim families to offer their apologies and show concern for their children's health. Greg now believes that the visits served to break down the stereotype of the corporate bad guy who runs over people on his way to profits. Odwalla boldly took on responsibility, and its response ultimately saved the company.

Let's not underestimate how important it was for Odwalla's senior leaders to involve all workers in shaping the direction of the firm. The next chapter illustrates further the difference between treating a worker like a hired hand and treating that worker as a valuable team member.

Chapter Five

Valuing the Worker

Principle Five

The worker will be treated as a valuable
team member, not just a hired hand.

Vital Signs

Does the company offer a generous equity or profit-sharing
program? To what lengths does the company go to preserve
jobs in times of economic downturn? Are periodic job
cuts made as part of a profit-taking strategy? Is employee
involvement in corporate governance encouraged? Are strong
retirement benefits offered? Is the wage gap separating management and employees reasonable? Does the company pay
a livable wage? Are employees at all levels brought into the
decision-making process? Is the right to unionize respected?
Do senior managers negotiate with unions and other worker
associations in good faith? Are employees paid for overtime
work? Are layoffs or retraining practiced during times of

transition? Is skills training readily available to all employees? Are workers given a clear path to advance their careers?

The corporate firm arose in the capitalist economy as the private possession of a small base of financiers. Workers were treated as a capital expense, much like physical plant and raw materials. Although Henry Ford was obviously a brilliant innovator at material production, he mirrored the mind-set of his day when he complained, "Why is it that I always get the person when what I really want is a pair of hands?"[1]

A free contract between workers and owners sounds ideal, yet power rarely distributes justice freely. The history of the twentieth century is filled with worker struggles to gain even the most basic rights. Child labor protection, safe factory conditions, health care provisions, minimum pay, and equal pay for equal work were not the fruits of corporate largesse. They were won only at great cost to organized workers.

We now have the opportunity to enter a new era in the owner-worker relationship. Workers up and down the corporate ladder aspire to be partners in the enterprise. Once they are treated like valuable team members, they start to view their own personal success as part and parcel with the company's success. This chapter holds up a few promising trends that are moving us in that direction.

It is foolish to look too far forward, however, when the legacy of the past remains such a vital force. The pursuit of basic worker rights is not over; we are still very much in a time of transition. The chapter begins, then, with entrenched assumptions about the worker's place in the firm. Even at a corporation as highly regarded as Wal-Mart, workers struggle to overcome the hired-hand treatment.

ALL WORK, NO PAY

Wal-Mart employees and former employees in twenty-eight states are waging legal battle against their employer, accusing the retail giant of cheating them out of overtime pay. Supervisors ordered them to continue working even after they punched out on the time clock, say Wal-Mart workers. In some cases, managers locked the store doors after closing time and prevented workers from leaving until the store had been readied for the next business day. It is not the first time that Wal-Mart has faced these accusations. In 2000, it paid $50 million to settle a class action lawsuit charging that sixty-nine thousand of its employees in Colorado had been forced to work off-the-clock.[2]

Overtime rules have been on the books in the United States since the 1930s. They require employers to pay anyone working over forty hours at a rate of time-and-a-half the standard hourly wage. The law also stipulates that employers cannot force workers to labor unpaid hours.[3]

Wal-Mart officials defend their company, pointing to corporate policies that explicitly forbid off-the-clock practices, in compliance with state and federal laws. Worker advocates acknowledge the written policy, but charge that corporate executives in practice apply such heavy pressure on local stores to avoid paying overtime that store managers see no other option than to demand off-the-clock labor. A senior Wal-Mart payroll executive revealed under court deposition that every store has to send corporate headquarters a daily report noting whether the store had exceeded its payroll limit. Store managers who fail to minimize overtime pay can be reprimanded or fired.[4]

Wal-Mart, the world's wealthiest corporation, with $220 billion in annual sales, is frequently lauded for its streamlined business model, and many of its innovative strategies are worthy of emulation. Its inventory system and distribution network, for example, are beyond compare in the retail industry. Its business acumen is paying financial dividends. While operating costs at the average retail store run at 20.7 percent of sales, and most giant retailers face an even higher cost-to-sales ratio (Sears Roebuck, for instance, sits at 24.9 percent), Wal-Mart holds its operating costs to an astounding low of 16.6 percent of sales.[5]

But let's look at the cost figures from another angle. One part of Wal-Mart's recipe for success involves resisting unionization at its stores while squeezing labor costs. Most hourly workers at Wal-Mart earn less than $8.50 an hour, which amounts to $17,680 a year for full-time employment.[6] That means a full-time employee at Wal-Mart is working under the official U.S. poverty level for a family of four.[7]

Lean and Mean

Executives of public companies meet with financial analysts every quarter to report their firms' performance. These days, you are almost guaranteed to hear them talk about the measures they have taken to make their firm lean and mean. Firing large numbers of workers used to be considered a last resort in times of declining market conditions, an admission of failure, or perhaps a necessary evil in times of technological change. Today, it is a badge of strong management.

The sorry plight of workers at the Providian Financial Corporation is a sign of the times. For much of the 1990s, Providian was a high-flying darling of Wall Street that had moved successfully into the business of providing credit cards to borrowers with shaky or limited credit histories. Once consumer default rates began rising with the economic downturn, however, the strategy backfired on the company.

Providian was also badly damaged by a series of class action lawsuits and irregularities in its financial reporting. In both 2000 and 2001, it paid out settlements to customers who accused it of deceiving them about fees and interest rates. Numerous customers say the company offered them a guaranteed savings rate yet were never told what interest rate they would be charged; others were marketed a credit card with a promise of no annual fee but forced them to buy credit protection. Introduced as court evidence during the legal battle were a series of company memos sent between executives that show a company bent on misleading its customers. "The problem is to squeeze out enough revenue and get customers to sit still for the squeeze," wrote Providian founder Andrew Kahr to other top managers.[8]

Sadly, it is Providian's workers who are paying dearly for their company's sins. Senior managers axed almost 45 percent of its workforce in 2002—a cut from about 13,200 employees down to 7,200 employees in less than twelve months. To impress the investment community that it is serious about getting lean and mean, Providian, not unlike many other large corporations, times its layoff announcements to coincide with its quarterly financial reports. A news clip in the *San Francisco Chronicle* speaks volumes:

Providian Financial Corp. said Tuesday that it is laying off an additional 1,300 employees in a continued effort to reduce the size of the company to match its new, downsized credit card business. The San Francisco company also reported a profit of $153.9 million on reduced revenue of $1.32 billion. . . .

Asked how the continued workforce reductions were affecting morale, [Providian] Chief Executive Officer Joseph Saunders said, "It obviously isn't uplifting." He said management was told by employees that they wished the continued cutting would be concluded swiftly. . . .

[Providian's profits] exceeded analyst estimates of a loss of a penny per share. "This was just awesome," said Charlotte Chamberlain, an analyst with Jeffries & Co. in Los Angeles who often has been critical of Providian's management. "I certainly never expected to see profit like this quite so soon."[9]

Although one could understand why a financial analyst would be thrilled by this apparent turnaround, the loss of six thousand jobs that made the results possible dampens our enthusiasm. The situation mirrors a troubling pattern. Workers are put at the bleeding edge of financial performance; when the numbers do not match expectations, workers are the first casualties. It strikes us as particularly unfair in the case of a Providian or a WorldCom, where senior managers violate the rules and put their firms in financial crisis, yet it is the workers who fall.

Since World War II, the corporation and its workers had an implicit agreement: if the company did reasonably well, workers could be more or less assured of job security and rising compensation. That's no longer the case; even very profitable companies lay off their workers or place a cap on wages and benefits.

Intel, for example, announced in July 2002 on a conference call with investors (along with its quarterly financials) that it would cut four thousand jobs. Although the company earned $446 million on $6.3 billion revenue for the quarter, its performance did not meet analyst expectations. Intel executives admitted that it did not know which part of the company would be hit with layoffs, but that it would make the necessary "cost-saving measures."[10]

Certainly, cutting jobs as a cost-savings measure is inevitable at times. I have worked with companies that have had no other option than to cut jobs because otherwise they would not make their payroll. But I have also seen firms use layoffs as a quick fix for solving problems that have nothing to do with payroll. Downsizing may buttress the financials in the short run, but it rarely makes a company more efficient or drives its profitability.

Alan Downs once was a corporate manager responsible for enacting sizable layoffs; he relates being in a strategy room at AT&T where the fate of employees was decided by moving their photographs around on a panel board. But he eventually soured on its benefits to a company's performance. He points out four myths that prop up its credibility among managers all the same:

Myth 1:   Downsized companies are leaner.

Myth 2:   Layoffs increase productivity.

Myth 3:   New, better jobs are being created.

Myth 4:   Downsizing increases profits.

To satisfy his curiosity, Downs did a careful analysis of business operations at major corporations both before and after massive downsizing. What he found was a broken trail of communication, stalled productivity, and battered morale.[11]

Workers Are Assets

At times when layoffs seem unavoidable, the story of Aaron Feuerstein, CEO of Malden Mills Industries in Lawrence, Massachusetts, offers an alternative path. Malden Mills has a strong global brand as the exclusive manufacturer of Polartec fabric. For his part, Feuerstein has become an icon for his treatment of his textile workers.[12]

Factories owned and operated by Malden Mills caught fire on the evening of December 11, 1995. News of the six-alarm fire reached Aaron as he arrived home from celebrating his birthday with a large gathering of friends and family. He raced over to the company site and saw a fireball consuming three of his primary plants. He immediately noticed that the fire had not progressed as far at a fourth, adjoining facility, the finishing plant. The finishing process is what distinguishes Malden Mills's products from other commodity fleece manufacturers. Aaron knew that to save the business from utter ruin, that plant had to survive.

But the prospects did not look good. The firefighters on the scene had given up on all four plants. "That's when my heroes stepped in," recounts Aaron. "Nearly thirty of my workers went into the finishing plant and fought the blaze all night long." At sunrise the next morning, the fire had died, and the fourth plant was still standing.

Aaron was seventy years old and a scion of a family-owned business. After the fire, no one in the business world would have faulted him for keeping the insurance money as his personal retirement fund. Then again, he could have used the tragedy as an excuse to take the company's manufacturing overseas to a country that would guarantee lower wages.

Instead, Aaron announced the next day that he would rebuild the plant atop the smoldering ashes in Lawrence. He also pledged to keep all three thousand of Malden Mills's workers on payroll for a month. When the first month ended, Aaron extended his voluntary salary payout for an additional two months and health benefits for six months. By the end of February, two and a half months after the fire, around 70 percent of the employees were back to work. By September, the new Malden Mills manufacturing facility was completely operational; practically every worker employed at the time of the fire had his or her job restored.

One might guess that the company had deep cash reserves to cover Aaron's generosity. In fact, Malden Mills was at grave financial risk after the fire. Insurance covered only three-quarters of the $400 million price tag of reconstruction. Add in that the calamity led to unavoidable delays in fulfilling customer orders, and the financial picture was dismal. So what moved Aaron to such lengths of generosity? "I simply felt an obligation to the entire community that relies on our presence here in Lawrence; it would have been an unconscionable act to put three thousand people out on the streets." Aaron is also quick to point out that the loyalty is reciprocal: his workers had risked their lives to save the finishing plant.

To dig itself out of a financial hole, Malden Mills had to be firing on all cylinders after relaunch. In the textile business, a manufacturer cannot afford to lose its market share; lost customers are not easily regained. Malden Mills's workers rose to the occasion. Before the fire, the finishing plant yielded 130,000 yards of fabric a week. After relaunch, production output ramped up to 230,000 yards per week. The company was saved.

Putting Out a Fleece

The world took notice of Aaron after the infamous fire. But his track record as a chief executive and owner reflect an abiding adherence to a labor philosophy that he expresses in a tidy slogan: "I consider my workers an asset, not an expense."

Malden Mills's roots go back to 1906, when Aaron's grandfather established a textile mill in the small town of Malden, Massachusetts. Aaron moved the company down the road to Lawrence in 1956 even as a large number of other New England textile mills were migrating to the U.S. South to find cheap labor. He believed his competitors were making a mistake: competitive advantage cannot be narrowed to the cost of labor. Aaron staked his future on keeping a highly skilled labor force. "If all you are after is cutting costs, you run the risk of losing superior quality," he asserts.

Aaron does not sugarcoat the fact that downsizing may be inescapable at times. A business leader, he stresses, cannot shirk the responsibility of keeping a company profitable. He points back to the late 1970s when the market for textile manufacturing collapsed. Malden Mills filed for bankruptcy protection, and he was forced to lay off hundreds of workers. Although no one was happy about the job losses, the workers understood; they respond to justifiable layoffs differently than they would to job weeding, says Aaron. "Layoffs necessitated by financial exigency do not break the workers' trust in the employer," he explains, "but if you use downsizing solely as a strategy to shave some expenses, then your workers resent it and may never forgive you for it."

The evidence speaks for itself. Although Malden Mills is a union shop, Aaron has never faced a worker strike. Its employee retention sparkles at nearly 95 percent.

Aaron restructured the company out of bankruptcy in 1981, shearing product lines that were losing money and pouring resources into research and development. The strategy paid dividends, as his research team came up with a series of lightweight, weather-resilient fabrics for outdoor sportswear branded under the label Polartec. Polartec became a fabric of choice among upscale retailers like Lands' End, L. L. Bean, Patagonia, and North Face. Malden Mills's sales grew to $400 million annually with retailers in more than fifty countries.

Aaron's Values: Outmoded or Enduring Business Principles?

○ A worker is an asset, not an expense.

○ Skilled labor offers a sharper competitive edge than cheap labor.

○ A business has a moral responsibility to sustain its community.

○ Workers accept justifiable layoffs but resent job weeding.

○ Management commitment yields worker loyalty.

○ Customers respond to quality and innovation above price.

○ Profit is only one among many values a company strives to maximize.

Rain Falls on the Just and the Unjust Alike

Like most other commodity industries, textiles pass through periodic financial cycles. The plentiful years of the 1980s and mid-1990s gave way to scarcity by the end of the century. A flood of cheaper goods produced overseas cut deeply into Malden Mills's sales. Revenues at the company dropped precipitously to $180 million in 2001, and earnings evaporated. Aaron was forced once again to file for bankruptcy protection.

Their boss on the brink of disaster, Malden Mills's workers once again returned his kindness. About one thousand union workers agreed to forfeit paid personal days in 2002 and freeze their salaries for two years for a company savings of nearly $2 million.

The company also benefited from a groundswell of grassroots customer support. Aaron receives letters from admirers around the world, some even enclosing small financial donations in the envelope. Sparked by this outburst of loyalty, the company launched a "Polartec Promise" campaign that urged consumers to buy products made with its fleece instead of lower-cost material manufactured overseas.

As its future hangs in the balance, Aaron is being pressed by creditors to transfer Malden Mills's production to cheaper labor markets. Although he may have no choice but to outsource some of his production, Aaron is not prepared to step aside and abandon his workers. "I won't hand this company over to people who believe that throwing out our workers and outsourcing manufacturing 100 percent is the only reasonable way for us to go," he says resolutely.

Aaron considers it a miracle that none of his major customers left the company once it went into Chapter 11 bankruptcy. Pragmatically, they have stuck with the company for a number of reasons. First, Malden Mills and its Polartec brand stand for integrity in the eyes of the public, and retailers want to be associated with that kind of reputation. Second, unlike cut-rate fleece textile manufacturers, Malden Mills puts resources into research and development, a strategy that has helped the company produce innovative, high-end fabrics. Finally, Polartec offers Aaron's retail partners a hedge against mass market merchants that push the price point of goods, not necessarily the quality.

Sadly, it may be out of Aaron's power this time to determine the destiny of Malden Mills. Creditors have their hooks deep into the company. Aaron is optimistic that everything will come up roses, and why not? He has already passed through fire.

PEOPLE DEVELOPMENT WITHIN THE CORPORATION

Whenever anyone tells me that a corporation cannot act with soul, I think of Aaron Feuerstein. It takes the moral fortitude of a prophet occasionally to shake us out of our limited vision of what's possible.

At the same time, Aaron's story points to the complexity of owner-worker relations. Even the most compassionate employer cannot guarantee worker security or compensation level. Companies grow, change, compete, succeed, and sometimes fail. Business is a risk venture, and that risk extends to the worker as much as it does to the owner.

Shaping a View of Employee Development

Chuck Fred has spent his career trying to come up with strategies to minimize the human cost of change within the corporation. He was a line manager at two major U.S. corporations when massive job layoffs were mandated from above. A few snapshots of his experience will set the context for discussing his notion of people development.

Chuck started his career as an aeronautics engineer at the Boeing Company.[13] During his ten years there, he watched the company go through the best of times and the worst of times. In the late 1980s, Boeing profited from an order backlog in the tens of billions of dollars. Fat with cash, it undertook a major recapitalization campaign, tearing down old facilities built during World War II and constructing new factories equipped with state-of-the-art machinery.

Chuck was assigned as general manager of one of the new plants that produced mechanical pieces to support an airplane engine bloc, known as engine ducting in the industry. No sooner had he assumed his post than he was confronted with a major challenge.

The U.S. government desperately wanted to strike a trade balance with Japan. A substantial volume of Japanese-designed automobiles was being manufactured in the United States. Boeing, the world's largest producer of commercial aircraft, could provide some symmetry to the manufacturing imbalance. The production of engine parts therefore was put on the list of possible candidates for an offset program. Boeing's senior management drew a line in the sand for the general managers responsible for factories: "If your production team cannot improve its efficiency by 25 percent and its overall quality performance, we will transfer your production overseas."

To reach his plant's targets, Chuck needed to train thousands of workers to learn new skills. He initially called on Boeing's corporate training team for help, but that proved a disappointment. "We were competing on a cycle where every day counted, while the trainers proposed to deliver ten-week programs based on learning methods that were fifty years old!" says Chuck.

He kicked the trainers out and together with his staff designed on-the-job skills training that would bring his crew up to speed. "We discovered that people can learn ten times faster than standard expectations of how long it would take to retrain a technical workforce," says Chuck.

Sadly, Chuck ran out of runway, as did many other plant managers. Senior management informed them that the company did not have the financial resources to retrain all of their workers. Most of Boeing's engine production was contracted out to Japan.

Chuck was not surprised by management's reticence to invest in retraining. Factories are treated almost entirely as an expense-driven line item in the manufacturing world. Because incremental expenses translate into a reduced profit margin, executives are reluctant to hand out a big allowance for retraining factory workers. Added to that, it's a rare executive who believes it is even possible to achieve a major skill redevelopment of an existing workforce. Instead, they go through the costly exercise of hiring new people to replace the now-outmoded workers. "It's a paradox: we hire students out of colleges as if they are proficient and ready to go, though every manager knows they're not, yet we aren't willing to retrain our own people," says Chuck.

When the global recession hit in 1992, Boeing embraced a remedy popular at the time: reengineering. At Boeing, it meant that many got "reengineered" straight out the factory door. Frustrated that the company once again was eliminating capable people with deep knowledge of the company's operation, Chuck resigned.

As the years passed, Chuck kept an eye on his former company. He was curious about whether Boeing could hire a new workforce to meet its reengineering strategy. "They went out and hired people they thought had the right skills," he reports. "But four years later, they found themselves in the exact same position." Technical changes accelerated, and the new people they had hired lost their proficiency. Boeing's senior management decided that they couldn't spend money retraining them and made more major layoffs, claims Chuck.

Not that he was feeling smug. By then, Chuck was living in a parallel universe. He had been hired to run a special project for U.S. West, the Ma Bell of the Rocky Mountains. U.S. West had embarked on an ambitious project in the mid-1990s to build a fiber network across the Rockies to meet the growing needs of Internet users. The operation put 9 billion conductor feet of fiber-optic cable in the ground across Colorado, Utah, and Arizona.

Putting cable into the ground was a familiar task for U.S. West workers, but splicing the ends of the fiber-optic fibers was not. For 125 years, technicians had been twisting two pieces of copper together. The fiber-optics conversion required a more specialized process: sitting in a humidity-controlled truck, microscope in hand, welding two tiny end pieces of glass together.

Chuck estimates that it would have taken two weeks to train a copper splicer how to do the work of a fiber-optic splicer; the corporate training department at U.S. West disagreed, projecting it would take six months. Fearing major expenses in retraining, U.S. West's senior management laid off a large contingent of its cable workers and outsourced the welding task to contractors that claimed to have proficient splicers.

Chuck was ready to tear his hair out: "The people who were let go understood the needs of our key customers and knew where all the cable was buried, yet we didn't have the vision to see how we could help them grow." He walked out the door with his workforce once more, his patience tapped out by the waste of human capital in yet another major corporation.

Making Promises You Can Keep

After Chuck left U.S. West, he made it his mission to change corporate attitudes toward worker competency. He has met with executives at over three hundred corporations to evaluate their worker training policies. Most of them feel stuck at a crossroads, he says. A big portion of their workers has the wrong skills, yet a training program in place is incapable of retraining them efficiently and affordably.

There's one question he usually asks senior managers: "What promises have you made to your customers?" He has discovered that most of them are unable to answer that question with any clarity. "And when they can't," says Chuck, "I can guarantee you that the company is not training its people the right way."

Who has not had the experience of placing a call to a corporation in response to a newspaper or television ad, only to find out that the person on the other end of the line knows nothing about the offer? Companies often unleash a marketing campaign to entice customers yet without the people in place who know how to deliver on the offer. In a service economy, the gap between promise and delivery is especially glaring.

Although most corporations have a training budget, Chuck finds that 90 percent of the training has nothing to do with

Aligning People Development and Customer Satisfaction

Here is a quick inventory for senior managers:

- What promises have you made to your customers?

- What skills do your workers need to fulfill those promises?

- How quickly do your workers need to be proficient in a new skill base?

- How will you prioritize resources to implement the necessary training?

- How do you minimize the operational cost and the human cost of the transition to a new skill base?

delivering on the promises that they make to customers. He looks back at his own experiences as a line manager at Boeing: "We had to produce the planes faster. I can't tell you how much money—probably $7 to $8 million—was available for management and supervisory training. But only a trickle of money was designated for training the people who had to deliver the product."

Chuck now works to help companies develop their own people. His clients include Home Depot, Starbucks, and ServiceMaster, all companies known for their excellence in customer service. He shares one of their secrets: they get their employees up to speed nearly twice as fast as their competition does. Top service companies aim to have new workers primed to perform at peak levels even before they begin acting as an official representative of their companies.

Workers perform better when they understand the promises that their company is making to the marketplace. They feel empowered to match their skills with the company's goals.

"Once employees can deliver on the company promise, they turn into great team members who want to improve the business operation," says Chuck.

LEARNING ON THE JOB

Workers are vulnerable when they do not have the right proficiency at the right time. Their best hedge against redundancy is to be gaining new skills constantly. Corporations that create a learning culture and offer their workers the resources to improve themselves minimize the human cost of reengineering or extreme swings in the market.

For a long time, one of my passions has been to find ways to reinvent corporate training. The potential of technology-enhanced learning intrigues me for that reason. Because technology can scale access, it enables companies to deliver critical information and skills training whenever and wherever possible. To increase learning opportunities across the company is fundamental, but it is not enough. Firms that have an excellent learning culture also meet three additional criteria:

- They merge learning with work.
- They expect workers to take responsibility for their learning path.
- They give workers an opportunity to advance their careers.

In the corporate world, United Airlines stands out as a company that achieves these goals. In fact, if it were not for its innovative use of skills training, one of the airline's most valuable operations may not have gotten off the ground.

United—and Apart—We Learn

United's training innovation began in late 1997 after the company's management drafted a plan to introduce a systemwide e-ticketing service. Gail Stockton, a senior training manager at United, was on the spot. She needed to figure out how to teach new protocols to twelve thousand customer service agents located in over 150 airport stations worldwide.[14]

Initially, Gail's team prepared a forty-hour conventional classroom workshop and tested the program with a few select groups of agents. The course instructors had to use a live ticketing system, so every ticket they issued in the training to demonstrate the e-ticketing process had to be cancelled immediately. As a result, ticket agents were given minimal hands-on practice, and once the class was over, they could not go back into the system to practice. Gail graded her early effort harshly: "It turned out to be a dismal failure."

Gail has a very pleasant demeanor, but it takes only a few minutes to realize she's a no-nonsense administrator. Her team was given a $3 million budget and a time frame of six months to get the job done. They decided to move the training out of the classroom and onto the computer. But first Gail had to convince top management that a $1.65 million investment in technology was going to pay off. "The secret of winning management's approval for a learning program is to make a very clear case of how training is going to impact operations," she shares.

Gail detailed the cost savings. Bringing every agent to one of its five national training hubs would have racked up prohibitive hotel and food expenses. More critical, it would have meant taking every employee off the job for a full week.

United estimates that 40 percent of its employee replacement hours is billed as overtime wages. Hence, each hour an employee spends in learning means huge outlays for the company.

Gail beefed up her proposal by projecting that 35 percent of United's customers would move to e-ticketing within two years. Given that e-ticketing saves the airline nearly fifty cents on every ticket sold, the rapid growth of the program would have a substantial impact on its bottom line. The executive staff liked hearing that the cost savings would be both immediate and recurring, and they approved the technology investment.

Flying Solo

United Airlines puts employees in control over their own careers by . . .

- Making a corporate commitment to retraining over replacing.

- Creating easy access to training courses.

- Tracking the certified skill set of each worker.

- Giving existing employees first crack at positions for which they are qualified.

- Pointing employees in the direction of training courses they need to reach their personal career goals.

Working with an outside multimedia group, Stockton's training team produced an e-ticketing simulation program for use on the computer. The star of the show became "E," an animated vowel that plays the role of the classroom instructor, flying across the screen in his open-cockpit plane as he passes along lessons. The interactive simulation also features video clips of actors staging customer interactions that the agents are likely to face on the job. Most important of all, the program provided a simulated system for booking and cancelling e-tickets.

The e-learning program launched in September 1998 cut the e-ticketing training course down to eighteen hours, a whopping 55 percent reduction in lost work hours. Equally important, proficiency levels soared: the best score among employees who took the classroom training was lower than the worst score among those who took the computer-based course.

Heather Young, a United sales agent stationed in Charlestown, West Virginia, has even more reason to appreciate United's flexible training program. If it weren't for the technology-delivered course work, she would have had to travel hundreds of miles to a regional United hub for her training. "I don't care how good the course is, I don't like to be away from home," Young says.

Largely due to the success of its agent retraining program, United's march toward e-ticketing accelerated. By December 1999, roughly 60 percent of its 7.1 million passengers booked using e-tickets.

The Sky's the Limit

A company with a strong learning culture encourages its employees to reach their potential. United Airlines pledges to its workforce that it will have first crack at any new job that comes up within the company. The onus is put on the employee, however, to pursue whatever training may be needed to qualify for the position.

Workers can visit a company intranet and match their own personal training portfolio with the qualifications of the new position. An employee who may fall short is directed to the requisite training courses offered at United or, if no in-house opportunities exist, at local colleges.

Gail admits that United's corporate training memory was in disarray until 1998. Detailed records of employee training were kept at local job sites, but once an individual transferred from one airport station to another, most traces of that employee's training history were lost. "We spent half our job trying to capture data, and it still was never up-to-date," she notes.

So Gail's corporate learning team implemented an educational tracking system. When employees log onto the system now, they can find out which courses are available to them, and if they've already started taking a course, it returns them to where they left off.

Although many corporations fear that a higher-skilled workforce will look for better jobs and better salaries elsewhere, United has proved the contrary to be true. Since it began taking a proactive approach to training about ten years ago, employee retention has risen markedly.

"Bottom line, I feel that this company cares about my career," shares Heather Young. How many corporate workers can honestly say that?

WORKERS AS OWNERS

To equip people to take control of their own job path already opens a new mind-set about a worker's potential in the company. Individuals have more power to choose the kind of contribution they will make to the enterprise and can set the horizon of their personal achievement. It is not much of a leap beyond to the idea that a worker can also become an owner of a firm.

"Those who contribute to the company should own it."[15] That's the maxim of a revolutionary experiment in corporate ownership that has won adherents across the United States. The movement emerged in a big way in the mid-1970s after the U.S. government established the tax deductibility of employer contributions to employee stock ownership plans (ESOPs). Over the past twenty-five years, the employee ownership movement has put approximately $65 billion in company assets into the hands of 10 million white- and blue-collar workers.[16]

Employee-owned companies come in all shapes and sizes. Most are small companies with fewer than five hundred employees, and only 22 percent are majority owned by the employees. The best known of the majority-owned companies is United Airlines, where employees have owned a 55 percent stake since 1994, obtained in exchange for $4.9 billion in wage and productivity concessions.[17]

A gorilla in the mist is Science Applications International Corp. (SAIC) of San Diego, which employs close to forty thousand people. Founded in 1969 as a consulting firm with government contracts, SAIC pulls in almost half of its $5.5 billion annual revenue today from commercial businesses like health care and energy. Current and former employees, several hundred of whom are millionaires based on their stock equity, own 90 percent of the company.[18]

An ESOP is a promising vehicle toward a more just distribution of riches. The owners of the company are the same people who by their sweat and tears make the firm more valuable. ESOPs stand out from other types of stock purchase plans because they foster long-term ownership of the company. Ninety percent of stock options, in contrast, are sold soon after they are exercised; in effect, options are treated like a delayed cash bonus.[19]

To clarify how an employee-owned company works, let's turn the spotlight on Chatsworth Products, a manufacturer of hardware support systems for the computer industry with headquarters in Westlake Village, California.

"When we launched our company, one of the first questions people asked me was, 'How long do you think it will take before you become an IPO?'" shares Chatsworth's president, Joe Cabral. "They were stunned by my reply: 'We never want to become an IPO because we don't want anyone outside of the company owning us.'"[20]

Chatsworth was established in 1991 when ninety employees from the Harris Corporation orchestrated a buyout of their business unit. Harris, a Fortune 500 communications equipment company, had targeted the unit for divestiture. While it tested the waters among interested corporate acquirers, Harris gave the workers an opportunity to create their own independent company.

Joe was head of the unit at the time. He explored a straight management buyout strategy but then evaluated alternatives. He discovered the ESOP option and immediately sensed that it was the perfect fit. The workers in his unit already were accustomed to a high degree of participation in decision making; an ESOP would endorse their chosen style of collaboration.

Despite the focus on worker participation, Joe emphasizes an important point that easily could be overlooked: for an ESOP to work, the management team must be fully on board. Some senior managers are threatened by the concept of workers as shareholders. By virtue of being the beneficiaries of a stock trust, employees de facto are granted many shareholder rights that could compromise total managerial control.

Joe believes that is the way a company should work: "We have become too accustomed to a labor-capital equation that is counterproductive," he says. "Instead of separating managers and owners from workers, let's bring them closer together. Why not turn workers into capitalists?"

To make the acquisition from Harris, a number of workers put at risk their accumulated retirement savings in a 401(k) rollover, and over forty individuals invested their own cash. They all gained stock equity in the new company.

Going forward, Chatsworth's ownership plan was open as well to all regular employees who met eligibility requirements. Employees are credited with company stock for each plan year in which they work a minimum of a thousand hours, with the actual allocation of stock based on a percentage of salary. Shares are directed to a worker's account and stay there as long as he or she stays at the company. The distribution policy comes into effect only once a worker leaves the company.

An independent appraisal firm sets the value of the company's stock once a year, and that value applies to distribution over the ensuing calendar year. While some employee-owned firms, and SAIC is among them, have an internal market for trading company stock, Chatsworth shares cannot be swapped.

Profit sharing is another important part of employee ownership at Chatsworth. Ten percent of the firm's pretax profits are distributed annually to full-time employees in the form of a cash payment. Everyone receives an equal share of the profits, whether that individual is the CEO or the janitor. "We believe that everyone was instrumental in creating the profit," explains Joe, "so let's share those slices equally." Some years, the profit-sharing check has come out to almost 25 percent of a factory worker's annual income.

The pride of ownership at Chatsworth is expressed by the company motto: "We're all in this together." In this age of feel-good-motivation-speak, maybe that message is altogether familiar. But Chatsworth has a company structure to back it up. Everyone in the company is tugging on one side of the rope.

In large corporations, it is not uncommon for operating units to be assigned their own performance goals and profit and loss, with job promotions and compensation riding on those factors. When a business unit takes an order, it will therefore tend to favor its own shop. Competition inside the company ensues, and turf wars and political fighting within the same corporation can get downright nasty. Too often, customers get caught in the crossfire.

The multiple operating units at Chatsworth do not face the same low-intensity conflict. Performance incentives are based on companywide goals, not those set for individual business units. When customer service representatives take orders at, say, the company's North Carolina shop, the representative can evaluate how best to fulfill the order in a way that meets that customer's needs. Emphasis is put on sacrificing parochial achievements for the benefit of the customer, which

Stimulating the Pride of Ownership

Chatsworth Products deploys five mechanisms:

- Generous distribution of company stock that stays inside the company until employee departs

- Annual profit sharing

- High levels of participation in decision making

- Aligning individual performance to the corporate bottom line

- Complete managerial transparency on financials and operations benefits total results. "Every time you create a box around a part of the company, you create a misalignment that will come back to hurt you," Joe argues.

Chatsworth has thrived under self-ownership. In the first decade after the buyout, the company saw its sales rise by more than 1,000 percent. Workers who began with Chatsworth in 1991 have watched their contribution to the ESOP account surpass the total value of their salary over that same period. "And they deserve it," Joe exclaims. "I'd much rather see it go to these folks than to investors on Wall Street who are basically gambling on a company's short-term prospects."

An employee-owned company operates in a world of paradoxes. Even among companies that encourage high levels of participation in decision making, the final buck for the tough decisions rests solely with the management. That responsibility becomes daunting when an industry is shrinking.

With intense compression in its sector, Chatsworth hit some major rough patches. The company had geared up its operation to meet the high demand for computer networking. Once that demand crashed, Chatsworth found itself with overcapacity. The company was forced to lay off more than 20 percent of its workforce in 2001, and the following year it closed one of its manufacturing plants, leading to even more job cuts.

These decisions were not a surprise. Chatsworth's managers had shared openly with the workforce their concerns as difficulties appeared and solicited innovative ideas for resolving the crisis. Nevertheless, layoffs eventually became inevitable.

Not only are layoffs an emotionally charged course of action, they take on an added strategic challenge for an ESOP. When employees are let go, the company has to fulfill the repurchase of their stock. Repurchasing can be paid out over as long as five years after distribution commences. Nonetheless, a significant job cut will mean a major hit on cash flow. For that reason, Chatsworth has judiciously reinvested 90 percent of its annual profits back into the company and was prepared.

Despite the downturn, Joe is optimistic that the company will grow when the market rebounds. He adds that he would not want to go through a downturn without an ESOP. "Our folks are doing everything imaginable to get the company turned around because they have a real stake in the future of this company," he says. "That translates into a lot of motivation and camaraderie."

This chapter has promoted a number of ways to enhance the role of the worker as a stakeholder in the corporation. In many respects, that argument is much easier to make than a parallel call to make the environment a corporate stakeholder.

The environment has no voice in managing a corporation. Nonetheless, it supplies many of the resources, the land, and the atmosphere necessary for all business to take place. Once those natural resources are depleted, no substitute can take their place. To give voice to the environment as a stakeholder is the agenda of the next chapter.

Chapter Six

Respect for the Environment

Principle Six

The environment will be treated as a silent stakeholder, a party to which the company is wholly
accountable.

Vital Signs

Does the company invest in, produce, or promote products
and services beneficial to the environment? Does the company work at creative pollution prevention programs, recycle, or
use recyclable parts? Are alternative fuels (natural gas, wind
power, solar energy, hydrogen) produced and promoted? Is
groundwater safety monitored? Does the company search for
ways to reduce and eliminate waste from its operations? Does
the company look for ways to source its products with organic materials? Does the company design for the environment?

Is the ratio of resource use to the production of goods and services measured? Is an environmental management system implemented? Is an open dialogue with environmental groups and other community stakeholders maintained? Are environmental limits identified and accounted for in planning? Does the company apply ecological auditing as it evaluates how it will invest in the future?

Monsanto enjoyed a monopoly on polychlorinated biphenyls (PCBs) production in the United States for nearly forty years.[1] PCBs are coolants used inside electrical equipment and have been shown in numerous medical studies to be potential carcinogens. For decades, Monsanto ran a cost-benefit analysis on its relationship to the rivers and streams of Anniston, Alabama. Should it continue its lucrative $22 million a year production of PCBs or risk public exposure for polluting the environment? The environment always came up on the short end of the ledger.

Now it appears likely that the chemical giant will be forced to make a balloon payment for its misdeeds. In February 2002, an Alabama jury found both Monsanto and a chemical division it spun off into a separate company, called Solutia, liable for negligence in the town of Anniston for having flushed tens of thousands of pounds of PCBs into nearby creeks and buried millions of pounds in a hillside landfill.

Many of the Anniston plaintiffs were found to have PCB levels in their blood twenty-seven times the national average. Although the town's residents did not learn about the PCB hazard until 1996, court documents proved that Monsanto knew about it for decades. In 1966, for example, Monsanto managers found that fish tossed into a local creek died within ten seconds, spurting blood and peeling skin as if they had been dropped into boiling water. Three years later, an internal company test found a fish in a nearby creek with seventy-five hundred times the legal PCB level. In both cases, the company chose to suppress the information.

In the end, Monsanto's own internal communications did the company in. A trail of documents, many labeled "CONFIDENTIAL: Read and Destroy," exposed a companywide complicity to maintain its monopoly of the PCB market regardless of health or environmental risks. A company committee formed to address the environmental hazards of PCB came up with only two strategic goals: "Permit continued sales and profits" and "protect image of . . . the corporation."

Monsanto likely will be forced to pay out millions, if not billions, of dollars in damages. The jury held the company liable on all six counts it considered: negligence, wantonness, suppression of the truth, nuisance, trespass, and outrage. Under Alabama law, a charge of outrage is rare, reserved for conduct "so outrageous in character and extreme in degree as to go beyond all possible bounds of decency . . . and utterly intolerable in civilized society." That's not the kind of rap on which a corporation wants to build its reputation.

The Environment Gains a Voice

In the not-too-distant past, environmental management was a matter of minimizing a firm's contribution to pollution. The company would steep itself in the regulations that pertained to its industry and make sure it stayed within the guidelines. The burden for keeping firms accountable for their environmental impact fell primarily on the shoulders of governmental agencies. How aggressively those agencies played that role would wax and wane with the political winds.

It is unlikely that a situation like Anniston would go undetected today, at least for such a long period of time. The environment has gained a new voice as a stakeholder. A potent swarm of public interest groups has emerged, sometimes working in concert with government agencies yet often moving beyond them. The National Wildlife Federation, for instance, puts out annually a highly publicized Toxic 500 list that features the worst corporate polluters. The "public enemies" that appear on the list may be targeted for protest and market boycotts.

Consumer groups practice a form of accountability as well. Organizations with names like the Green Consumer Guide provide people the data they need to make informed ecological choices. The "green" consumer wants to know whether a company's products, its manufacturing methods, and its policies respect the integrity of the environment. They expect the company to hold their suppliers accountable to the same standards.

Managing consumer expectations can get a bit complicated, as my friend John Sage reminds me. John left a highly successful career in the technology industry to start a coffee company. He brewed his company, Pura Vida Coffee, with high ideals: 100 percent of its net profits are directed to better the lives of street children in Costa Rica.[2]

Pura Vida is a for-profit company, however, and John operates it as such. He offers premium coffee that can rival any other supplier in quality and cost. John has discovered that organic and shade-grown (a method with less ecological impact) coffee is important to some of his consumers. Still others ask for fair trade coffee that guarantees an equitable wage to the independent farmers who grow and pick the coffee.

To remain competitive, John offers a range of products to his consumers at the price points that correspond to their production costs. Some of his largest customers are not willing to pay the higher cost for his "triple seal" coffee: fair trade, organic, and shade grown. The customers who prioritize these values will pay more. All the same, John is surprised to be criticized occasionally for not being pure enough. He is asked, for example, why he isn't 100 percent organic or doesn't buy only fair trade coffee.

John's philosophy is to be completely transparent about his products and let consumers vote with their purchases. In practice, his customers have become his partners in moving Pura Vida toward more organic sourcing. Since its introduction two years ago, triple-seal coffee now represents more than 50 percent of Pura Vida's total sales volume.

It benefits a company to sustain an ongoing dialogue with all manner of stakeholders. If it does not stay abreast of their expectations, the ground may shift one day, and the company will not be prepared to keep its feet. A Canadian timber company, MacMillan Bloedel, can attest to how risky that position can be.

MANAGING STAKEHOLDER EXPECTATIONS

MacMillan Bloedel built its early fortune along the coast of British Columbia.[3] During the 1930s, its Franklin River camp boasted the largest logging operation in the world. It was here that Canadian loggers were introduced to the chainsaw and the logging truck fleet. The company worked quietly according to its own rules, delivering as much timber as possible at low cost to the sawmill gates.

But the world was changing in the 1980s, and MacMillan Bloedel was unprepared. The company's practice of clear-cutting rare forestlands on the coast of British Columbia made it a top target in the standoff between timber companies and an international environmental movement.

MacMillan Bloedel inadvertently lit the fuse with a plan to log Meares Island, a landmark sacred to aboriginal groups. The Nuu-chah-nulth Nation sought a court injunction to protect the heart of its traditional territory. The state court agreed to halt the logging pending the outcome of treaty negotiations. The decision gave nonnative environmental groups hope that conservation victories were possible in British Columbia's coastal regions.

Initially, MacMillan Bloedel relied on conventional avenues for resolving its disputes with public stakeholders over logging. Since the company was leasing forestland from the provincial government of British Columbia, it directed native and environmental groups to take up their complaints with the government. Once that attempt to sidestep the fracas failed miserably, the timber company turned to litigation. The company expected the courts to enforce the legal harvesting rights it had been granted by the state government.

But once the situation became globalized, this approach proved inadequate as well. A coalition of public interest groups led by Greenpeace and the Rainforest Action Network initiated a market campaign to boycott its products internationally. They also rallied environmental activists from around North America to trek to Clayoquot Sound. In the summer of 1993, over eight hundred protesters were arrested in the largest single campaign of civil disobedience in the history of Canada.

MacMillan Bloedel had reached a dead end. It concluded that it could no longer expect the government and the courts to resolve stakeholder conflicts. It needed to enter into direct dialogue with its adversaries.

MacMillan Bloedel hired Linda Coady to expand its problem-solving toolkit. She was a veteran of the timber industry, having cut her teeth on public policy and government relations. The new vice president of environmental issues took the job assuming that her employer was doing the right thing and that straightforward solutions were achievable. Over the next two years, she engaged the company's stakeholders in extensive dialogue. To her surprise, she came to appreciate their point of view, and the complexity of the issue deepened for her. "I discovered that my company wasn't necessarily in the right," confesses Linda.

A zero-sum game occurs when two opponents can accept only a single outcome: the complete and utter defeat of their adversary. By the mid-1990s, MacMillan Bloedel and the environmental movement were posed in a classic zero-sum game. Neither side had any other strategy than to continue pouring more resources into the struggle.

To break the impasse, Linda decided to advocate for conservation forestry within her company. She had been persuaded that clear-cutting up and down wide swathes of a mountain was ecologically disastrous and a poor business practice as well. Linda told the president of MacMillan Bloedel her plan with characteristic wit: "I know I was hired to work with our loggers to fight Greenpeace, but it turns out that I'm working with Greenpeace to fight with our loggers."

Understandably, many of her work colleagues saw her as a traitor. Managers with budget line responsibility told her that new harvesting methods would undermine commercial margins. The unions said dispensing with clear-cutting would cost jobs. Yet Linda persisted.

She did sense momentum moving in her direction. Because of the negative publicity and mass protests, many MacMillan Bloedel workers were not feeling good about their jobs. Children of loggers were coming home upset because they were having debates in school about their parents' livelihood.

All the same, Linda found it more difficult to build consensus inside the company than with those outside the company gates. Most insiders have a vested interest in the status quo, which lowers their appetite for innovation and risk taking. "It's not easy going to managers with a payroll to meet or a customer to satisfy and ask them to change the way they think about forest conservation," she says. Linda then adds with a laugh: "It becomes that much harder when you tell them that they have to incur all the additional costs."

Sometimes good timing is as important as good planning. Just as Linda resolved to campaign for conservation as an insider, the MacMillan Bloedel board of director brought in a new CEO, Tom Stephens, to restructure the company. Weeks after his arrival, Stephens instructed Linda and the company's chief forester to put together a team of people and gave them a mandate: "In ninety days, put some recommendations on my desk how we can move wood from the hill to the mill in a way that will be recognized as environmentally responsible and still makes us money."

Besides being a no-nonsense administrator, Stephens brought a new philosophy to MacMillan Bloedel. He told his managers that the company had to go beyond the law to address social expectations. His rule of thumb is that the law is five years behind deeply felt social values. If a company ignores those values, it may lose its social license to operate.

In the mid-1990s, the timber industry in British Columbia thought the environmental movement represented an extreme position. Loggers were surprised to discover that many of the sentiments of the environmental movement (though certainly not all) represented a rising mainstream of social values.

Once the new CEO laid down his mandate, the battle came in-house at MacMillan Bloedel. Linda reports that her committee had lots of good fights, but eventually the team came up with a series of new methods for sustainable harvesting. The team took the proposals to outside stakeholders—native groups, the government, and environmental organizations—and then adapted the model to reach consensus. Finally, an agreement was reached that satisfied all parties.

The most publicized change was to end clear-cutting. MacMillan Bloedel pledged to move to a variable-retention method, which leaves standing groups of trees as a habitat for forest life, from birds and bugs to lichen and cougars. A number of other experimental practices in forest management also surfaced. "The public clamor that followed our decision makes it look as if MacMillan Bloedel underwent a radical transformation," says Linda. "But we actually looked at our risks, did a cost-benefit analysis, and made a totally rational management decision."

Linda claims that the real revolution happened inside the company. The process forced MacMillan Bloedel's culture to become more adaptive. She offers an example: "If I'm the logging division manager, is it my job to ensure that there is a

Ten Steps for Moving Away from Polarized Environmental Conflict

1. The company and environmental groups realize that neither side can completely defeat the other, but they can seriously damage the other.

2. Both sides recognize that the conflict is structural.

3. Pressure is applied from the marketplace and the general public to change the stalemate.

4. Both sides internally reach the conclusion that the status quo is no longer acceptable.

5. Individuals on both sides are willing to step out, take risks, and act as bridges.

6. Both sides realize that it is possible to work together on some substantive issues despite continuing disagreement on other substantive issues.

7. Each side forms its own internal alliances for change.

8. Both sides reach agreement on the need for a broader range of strategies and options.

9. Steps are taken to build trust; the individuals and groups involved will do what they say they will do.

10. Whatever you think the time frame is, double it, and then extend it by mutual agreement.

Source: Adapted from L. Coady, "Engaging Across Boundaries: Dynamics That Drive Change in Stakeholder Relationships" (paper presented at New Terms of Engagement Conference, Simon Fraser University Center for Innovation in Management, Vancouver, B.C., Apr. 2002).

fifteen-meter forested buffer retained along each side of a stream? Or is it my job to ensure that logging doesn't damage the quality of the habitat in the area of the stream? There's a big difference. The former approach is complying with the rules; the latter approach is about effective outcomes. At MacMillan Bloedel, we began to shift our mentality from product to process."

When Weyerhaeuser acquired MacMillan Bloedel in 1999, Linda Coady kept her job; she was too valuable an asset for a timber company to let go. In fact, in order for the American-owned Weyerhaeuser to gain approval for the acquisition of a Canadian company, it had to commit itself to follow through on the sustainable forest management that had been initiated at MacMillan Bloedel.

Building a Sustainable Business

This chapter has focused thus far on conflicted relationships that can exist between corporations and stakeholders who defend the environment. Let's shift gears now and investigate how conservation and economic development can work hand-in-hand.

The most widely used term for merging business and ecological concerns is *sustainable development*. It is still a very politicized notion, however. For the more militant environmental activist, sustainability might mean a low-tech future that would take us back to the agrarian age. Most mainstream environmental groups, though, realize that conservation and development are not so much in conflict as interdependent. They are engaging in dialogue with corporate strategists to come up with sustainable business models that appreciate the connectedness of humans, technologies, and natural resources.

To illustrate how an enterprise can convert ecological principles into a viable business model, let's take a close look at Stonyfield Farm. The fact that the company is now a part of the Groupe Danone conglomerate makes its case all the more intriguing.

Treating the Environment Like a Stakeholder

Groupe Danone, a worldwide supplier of dairy products, beverages, and cookies, is in a dogfight to lead the surging yogurt market in the United States.[4] Its U.S. division, Dannon, once ruled the American market, but its market share has slipped. Its competitors are especially savvy in reaching out to consumers concerned about a healthy lifestyle.

Natural foods are filling up space on America's grocery shelves. Once considered the province of a tiny core of countercultural waifs, natural foods today appeal to a mainstream audience. The U.S. market for organic yogurt alone grew a whopping 43 percent in 2001, with retail sales approaching $30 billion annually.

Danone had to admit to itself that it did not fully understand this niche. The French conglomerate had limited experience sourcing its products with organic ingredients and did not have a close relationship with organic consumers. To its credit, Danone realized it could not simply advertise its way to a green reputation.

Rather than squander resources on a hit-and-miss experiment, Danone bought a 40 percent stake in Stonyfield Farm, a small American company headquartered in Londonderry, New Hampshire, with a mighty brand. Stonyfield, with roughly $85 million in annual sales, became America's fastest-growing yogurt company by promoting all-natural and certified organic yogurt.

While Danone gained a foothold in a surging market, Gary Hirshberg, the CEO of Stonyfield, found a global platform. Gary has dedicated his life to building a company that, in his own words, "can change the world." Despite the spotty record of corporations in the past, he believes they have the potential to bring leadership to ecological stewardship. "Let's put it this way," says Gary. "If the world's business communities don't embrace the goal of a sustainable earth, it will never happen."

Making a Stand

When he was in his early twenties, Gary did not want anything to do with business. Born and raised in New Hampshire, he was mortified to witness the gradual slide of the southern half of the state into a congested suburb of Boston. In a way, he felt personally responsible; his father, and grandfather before him, had owned three shoe factories that had contributed to the urban sprawl. Determined to look for alternatives to industrial models of development, he took up environmental studies in college. After graduation, he ran a nonprofit institute promoting alternative energy sources and ecologically sustainable farming. That's not your typical CEO resumé.

But there was never any doubt that he was a spirited entrepreneur. In fact, he soon became frustrated with the constraints of his nonprofit. Its reach to the public was nominal, resources were strained, and he spent a big chunk of his time panhandling just to keep the institute afloat.

The turning point of his career occurred at the Epcot Center in Florida, of all places. Visiting his mother, a senior buyer for Epcot, he bumped into a Kraft-funded land exhibit demonstrating how food would be grown in the future. That scenario was precisely what Gary was developing at his institute, yet with a very different view of how the future should unfold. "The exhibition's message was, 'We'll keep mining the earth for fossil fuels; you keep buying the Velveeta cheese and leave the rest to us,'" says Gary, who has a penchant for dramatic language.

He was horrified by Kraft's vision and even more appalled to learn that nearly twenty-five thousand people were paying to visit the Kraft exhibit each day. That was around the total number of visitors that would come to his institute for an entire year. "I realized that to make an impact on the future of food production on this planet, I had to become Kraft foods," he says.

Despite his grand scheme, Stonyfield Farm launched with little fanfare in 1983. Gary and his partner, Samuel Kaymen, one of America's influential thinkers on organic farming, launched the company on a dairy farm with a few Jersey cows and Samuel's own yogurt recipe. Early on, Gary and Samuel did everything from milk the cows to deliver the products.

Gary admits underestimating how hard it would be to run a cash-positive operation. "I was tired of having my palm face-up at my nonprofit, so I saw building a business as breaking out of that rut," he says, breaking into a chuckle. "The joke was on me, because I spent the next ten years of my life constantly raising capital." His efforts did pay off, though, and the company soon outgrew the dairy farm.

Stonyfield set high standards for its products long before a large consumer demand for organic foods surfaced. From the start, the company wanted to be known for offering yogurt that is free from artificial ingredients and loaded with probiotic bacteria. Stonyfield built a supplier network of New England dairy farmers who refuse to use hormones to boost production, even though it makes the company's sourcing costs more expensive.

Stonyfield directs 10 percent of its annual net profits to its own Profits for the Planet Fund, which makes grants to environmental projects that protect and restore the earth. Most of the investments are strategic; a successful applicant has to show how its efforts will directly benefit Stonyfield's mission. The company donates funds, for example, to environmentally friendly packaging research and gives dairy farmers grants to change over their methods of production.

From production to marketing, the company treats the environment like a stakeholder. The rationale is simple: healthy food can come only from a healthy planet. Stonyfield aligns its brand to this relationship and continuously reinforces that message to its customers. Its best messenger is the soapbox that holds the yogurt itself. Each lid of yogurt serves as a mini-billboard for a specific environmental cause.

Stonyfield spearheaded a campaign in the fall of 2002, in tandem with the popular hosts of *Car Talk* on National Public Radio, asking Americans to drive more fuel-efficient cars. "LIVE LARGE, DRIVE SMALL" appeared in bold letters on every lid of Stonyfield yogurt. "We should aim to drive the smallest car in the class; not everyone needs a sport utility vehicle," says Gary, filling in a few more details.

The campaign shows great conviction, but doesn't Gary worry about turning off some of his customers? After all, a lot of suburban families who drive SUVs fall squarely into his consumer demographic. "Sure, I'm going to upset a lot of them," he acknowledges. "But over the twenty years we've been in business, we have never backed off from tackling tough ecological or social causes. I think our customers actually respect us for making a stand."

Seeding a Legacy

A big part of a leader's job is to inspire workers to care deeply about the mission of the company and to connect their jobs to its execution. Gary and his sister, Nancy, a senior manager at Stonyfield, created a corporate legacy program for that very end. The program arranges a regular roster of speakers—everyone from dairy farmers struggling to operate a family farm to global warming experts—to run workshops for employees during the workday. Every Stonyfield employee is asked periodically as well to take part in a retreat that focuses on the values of the company.

Gary believes in worker education, but experience has taught him that a firm's priorities need to be reinforced with tangible financial rewards. Workers receive a cash bonus each year the company reduces the amount of disposable waste it produces relative to what can be recycled. They are rewarded even more if energy use decreases or if water use per pound of production drops. Gary reports that the cost savings of these conservation measures run in the six figures annually. The fact that over 60 percent of Stonyfield's waste comes out as recyclables, never to see a landfill or an incinerator, is further testament to the success of the program.

"Some of my employees probably think I'm a bit loony," says Gary. "But even if they don't buy into my concerns for global warming or fully organic products, they can't discount the reality that we are about a different way of doing business."

Stonyfield Farm's Drive to Environmental Excellence

○ Source all products with natural ingredients, and move progressively toward being 100 percent certified organic.

○ Assemble a network of suppliers who agree to refrain from using hormones in their milk production.

○ Support family dairy farms whenever possible.

○ Link year-end cash bonuses for employees to companywide conservation in the use of material waste, energy, and water.

○ Be carbon neutral: invest in carbon offsets that absorb as much carbon dioxide as the company contributes to global warming.

○ Direct 10 percent of net profits annually to nonprofit ecological groups that potentially will enhance the company's mission.

○ Embed the company's marketing and communications with messages that promote a healthy individual and a healthy planet.

○ Offer a steady diet of educational events to help employees stay focused on the company's mission and values.

With the Danone investment, a number of critics charged that Gary and company had sold out and would gradually drift away from the principles that had guided the business thus far.[5] As noted above, Danone bought a 40 percent ownership stake in Stonyfield. It has the right to buy the remaining nonemployee stock in 2004, which would give it more than 50 percent equity in Stonyfield. Danone can buy the whole company if and when Gary decides to sell his ownership position.

Can a major global corporation tolerate the quirky policies and uncompromising social commentary that distinguishes

Stonyfield? The chairman and CEO of Danone, Franck Riboud, seemed to answer that question in a press call announcing the deal: "Stonyfield represents an ethic that we have to adopt if we're going to be successful in this new century." Commenting on that statement, Gary says wryly: "Yes, that's absolutely true, but the reason Danone can say that is because we have shown that you can make money living out that ethic."

Although he has great respect for Danone, Gary does not plan to lose control of the Stonyfield agenda. He negotiated a governance structure that would give him the right to appoint three of the five board seats as long as he remains at the helm of the company. The only way he can lose effective control of the company is to be fired, and the terms of his dismissal are specified to require two consecutive years of highly erosive decline to the bottom line.

The fact that Danone would enact such an unorthodox deal is testimony to both Danone's vision and the strength of the Stonyfield brand. Gary firmly believes that the new partnership is the right vehicle for Stonyfield to gain in stature while remaining loyal to the growing base of consumers who support organic and natural products. "To move the corporation in the direction I want it to go, it's critical to prove a business case that an environmentally and socially responsible company can turn a healthy profit."

Saving Costs as Well as the Planet

Gary Erickson has a goal to reduce Clif Bar's "ecological footprint on the planet" (see Chapter One). In that same vein, we can appreciate Stonyfield Farm's efforts to source organic materials in its products, reduce its waste of energy and water, and increase its use of recyclables. Although it may not make for exciting theater, it is in this area of eco-efficiency that some of the most important advances in sustainable development are being made.

Many large corporations are redesigning their manufacturing processes to ensure clean, efficient, and therefore cost-effective production. An eco-efficiency program established at SC Johnson Wax in 1990, for example, cut the company's manufacturing waste by half and reduced virgin packaging waste by 25 percent, while production rose by more than 50 percent. The company's largest plant mines methane gas from a nearby landfill and recaptures organic vapors from process lines to obtain one-third of its energy needs; another plant continuously reuses 95 percent of its wastewater so that it is never discharged. SC Johnson Wax has realized more than $20 million in annual cost savings from these measures.[6]

It may come as a surprise that big corporations are at the cutting edge of eco-efficiency. Small- and medium-sized enterprises tend to be less confident of the financial benefits of eco-efficiency and are more likely to believe that they lack the resources to make the requisite changes in their operations. But a study of five hundred smaller enterprises across various industrial sectors shows that pollution prevention does indeed benefit financial and operational performance at smaller firms.[7]

I'm always fascinated to learn how individuals introduce innovation in a company and overcome resistance to their efforts. Anita Burke's story fits that billing. She went to the Shell Oil Corporation to stimulate fresh thinking about sustainability and break new ground in eco-efficiency practices. To set the stage for Anita's work, here is a recap of one major incident that led Shell to turn in this direction.

Sustainable Development as a Hedge on the Future

In 1995, Greenpeace discovered that the British government and members of the European Union had granted permission for Shell to tow a heavily contaminated oil installation out into the North Atlantic and sink it in six thousand feet of water. The Brent Spar had been used as a loading buoy and storage tank for crude oil for fifteen years until it was decommissioned in 1991.[8]

Greenpeace activists boarded the station to buy some time while calling for mass demonstrations and a market boycott. Shell bled millions of dollars as the campaign gained sympathy across Britain and the rest of Europe. Some of Shell's subsidiaries lost as much as 40 percent of their sales virtually overnight.[9] The tension heightened after a Shell station in Germany was firebombed (an action that Greenpeace condemned).

Although the Brent Spar did not sink, Shell's reputation did do a nosedive. Its own opinion surveys showed a widening breach in public trust that depicted the company as callous to the health and welfare of the community.[10] In that split second that a driver is passing a number of competing gas stations, an oil company does not want the image of a major polluter to pop into the consumer's mind. Shell realized that to operate and compete in a world of unprecedented scrutiny, it had to change the way it did business.

Sustainability at Both Ends of the Pipe

Anita Burke joined Shell in 1999 to flesh out a business case for sustainable development.[11] Although she advises corporate strategy teams at Shell's headquarters in the Hague, Netherlands,

Anita works primarily with Shell Canada. She views the Canadian unit as an incubation lab because it is small enough to allow for the speedy implementation of new projects yet big enough to house the key elements of Shell's global portfolio. Anita typically works closely with each of Shell Canada's business units on plans to integrate sustainability into its operations.

Anita has a deep background in environmental stewardship. She was raised in the wilderness lands of Idaho and Alaska. After university studies in physics and environmental studies, she kicked off her career in the oil industry. She tackled hazardous waste management long before it was a hot political issue. "In those days we had so few environmental regulations in Alaska, most people had never heard of hazardous waste," says Anita.

Public concern rose dramatically with the *Exxon Valdez* oil spill in Alaska's Prince William Sound in 1989. Anita was recruited to manage the contract with Exxon for the disposal of waste materials. She directed teams to remove tons of dead wildlife and oil-tainted beachfront. This experience left a lasting impression on her. She resolved to do everything in her power to help oil companies rethink the way they do business.

When she arrived at Shell, Anita and a group of senior managers took a hard look at their company in relation to global trends. Anita notes that it was not just the Brent Spar incident that caused Shell to rewrite its operating manual. The managers saw a world where 80 percent of the population lacks an adequate place to sleep at night and an insufficient diet. People's desires for a better living and the rise of global markets would move the planet inexorably toward economic development, and energy would play a major role in that development. Anita reports that the managers looked at each other and said,

"We damn well better figure out how we're going to play in those new ventures, because it certainly won't be fueled by crude oil."

A finite supply of natural resources puts boundary conditions, that is, limits, on every corporation. Once the Shell managers conceptually placed their company inside those boundaries, Anita explains, they realized that the company had no choice but to search for alternatives that it did not then have. But the transition will not happen overnight. In the meantime, the energy market will continue to operate in a carbon-constrained environment. As Shell pours resources into researching alternative energy sources, it also has to make dramatic moves toward efficiency and conservation. Those conclusions, Anita reports, were her marching orders.

Anita is as pragmatic about sustainable development as she is visionary. While her goal is to change the values at the heart of a corporation, she concentrates on establishing new systems. "About 90 percent of the people working in the industrial area are engineers," she explains. "They act more soulfully once their system conditions free them up to do so."

At a very early stage, Anita strives to help individual business units become more interconnected. Each unit needs to be aware of the operational impact outside its own domain. As an example, Anita points to an oil refinery in Bakersfield, California, where she urged senior engineers to make collective decisions around a waste problem. "I knew they got it when I heard them say, 'Hey, we can't think about this problem just from our end of the pipe; we have to talk to purchasing about changing the chemicals that are being poured in at the front end of pipe.'"

On paper, that may seem like common sense. Anyone who has worked in a large corporation, however, knows that

Anita Burke's Step Ladder to Sustainability

1. Capture the hearts and minds.
   Provide internal education on sustainable development (SD).
   Set up an SD network between business units.
   Integrate SD practices into personnel training.

2. Welcome to the machine.
   Make SD a key factor in how the company invests in its future.
   Develop metrics for key performance.
   Assess the life cycle of each of the company's products and
     services.
   Set up environmental management systems.
   Implement pollution prevention and waste reduction in the most
     obvious places.

3. Take the leap.
   Support SD experiments and innovation.
   Use the by-products and wastes of one group as inputs for
     another.
   Improve the ratio between resource use and the production of
     goods and services.
   Design for the environment: prevent problems before they
     arrive.
   Engage in environmental cost accounting: value environmental
     assets.
   Engage in supply chain auditing: approve suppliers on the basis
     of their verifiable environmental record.

4. And how are we doing?
   Open up to external communication; set up an Internet site for
     public feedback.
   Engage external shareholders in dialogue around the environ-
     mental impact of its products.

Source: Adapted from Anita Burke, "The Business Case for Sustainable
Development," unpublished manuscript.

individual business units generally coexist like feudal fiefdoms in a loose alliance. In contrast, Anita urges units to operate like an ecosystem: adaptive, interdependent, self-sustaining, letting the old die so that a new thing can live.

Because the ecosystem is the result of 3.5 billion years of natural selection and succession, Anita believes it can teach us a great deal about efficiency in the production process. Zero emissions, for instance, depends on the efficient use of by-products from one part of the production cycle to be used as inputs for another part of the cycle. Once the loop is complete, by-products and waste are converted to resources and products.

At every point that an operation in the company does not close the loop, it is losing money. For that reason, Anita makes it very clear to Shell managers that sustainable development goes directly to the bottom line. She often opens a meeting with the managers of a business unit with a challenge—for example, "You guys have a fiduciary responsibility to our shareholders, and yet we have found 25 percent of their returns going out a pipe because we have chosen not to look at things from a sustainability window."

On a much broader scale, Anita and her team at Shell are designing a set of financial rules for valuing the atmosphere, rivers and lakes, soil, and other key natural resources. The ultimate plan is to restructure Shell's internal accounting system and investment strategy to incorporate these valuations. Shell already is including the cost of carbon in its investment decisions, one of only a handful of major corporations in the world to do so.

Here's how the ecological auditing process works in the most basic terms. The allowable concentration of carbon dioxide in the atmosphere at some point is a finite unit measure-

Corporate Goals for Sustainability and the Strategies to Accomplish Them

Goal: Social license to operate

Strategy: Pollution control and compliance

Goal: Best in class

Strategies: External stakeholder participation, environmental management systems, pollution prevention

Goal: Class of our own

Strategies: Sustainability a key factor in future strategic planning, products designed with environmental impact in mind, integrated management systems

Goal: Full sustainable development

Strategies: Preservation of natural resources, environmental accountability, explicit mainstreaming of environmental targets

Source: Adapted from A. Burke, *Operationalizing Sustainable Development* (Vancouver, B.C.: Shell Canada, 2000).

ment; beyond a certain tipping point, catastrophic destruction takes place. Because these units are finite, they have a value. The right to emit those units also implies a determined cost. It is not hard to imagine a commodities market one day trading these valuable units. That essentially was the Kyoto proposal, which was not ratified. But even if Kyoto-style guidelines do not come into play, other boundary conditions in the international market will emerge because atmospheric limits are not a mere hypothesis but a reality.

Economies put price tags on nature every day. Land use, for instance, involves implicit assumptions about value even when no dollar figure is assigned. New York City found it could avoid spending $6 to $8 billion on the construction of new water treatment plants if it were to protect an upstate watershed that performs purification naturally. Based on this economic assessment, the city invested $1.5 billion in land surrounding its reservoirs, a move that will not only keep its water pure at a bargain price but also enhance recreation, wildlife habitat, and many other ecological benefits.[12]

The repercussions of natural resource valuation are already buried in the budget of every company. Shell has chosen to make those costs more explicit. It will benefit from evaluating closely its impact on nature and adapting to its cycles in ways that are sustainable. "If we don't start applying sustainable development tools to our decision making now," Anita emphasizes, "then the businesses we want to launch in five to ten years aren't going to fit the boundary conditions that will exist at that time."

As the next chapter shows, boundaries shift in the social world as surely as they do in the physical universe. The population is increasingly diverse in most Western nations. Savvy corporations stay attuned to these changes and adapt with an eye to the future.

Chapter Seven

Equality and Diversity

Principle Seven

A company will strive for balance, diversity, and
equality in its relationships with workers, customers,
and suppliers.

Vital Signs

Does the company's workforce reflect the faces of the community? Are existing employees given every chance to apply for newly created positions? Are women and minorities represented among the company's executive management and directors? Is equal pay given for equal work? Are employment opportunities open to the disabled? Are minority clients and consumers fairly treated? Are promotions based on merit? Does everyone have equal access to the resources they need to fulfill the company's mission? Do underrepresented communities have a direct channel to voice concerns with senior management? Is there a bias against older employees? Does the company solicit procurement bids from women- and minority-owned enterprises? Are strong family benefits plans offered, including domestic partnership options? Do customers of every background feel welcome? Are markets in underrepresented neighborhoods aggressively pursued?

Barbara Campbell anticipated an enjoyable day with her family when they headed out for a meal at the Cracker Barrel in Wilson, North Carolina. When they arrived at the restaurant, the family requested a seat in the smoking section. Despite the fact that several tables in the smoking section appeared to be available, Barbara and her six family members, all African American, were ushered to a small table behind a partition in the nonsmoking section. A Cracker Barrel waitress brought them drinks and nothing else. When Barbara asked for ice in her drink, the server cleared the table of all the family's drinks and never returned. The family finally left after ninety minutes without having been served a meal.

Barbara is now a plaintiff in a $100 million class action lawsuit accusing the Cracker Barrel restaurant of widespread discrimination against black customers. America's oldest and largest civil rights group, the NAACP, has added its moral authority to forty-one other plaintiffs in the suit filed in a federal court in Georgia. "I marched with Dr. [Martin Luther] King," Barbara says, "and it concerns me that my grandchildren might have to endure that same struggle."[1]

Cracker Barrel, based in Lebanon, Tennessee, is one of the largest restaurant chains in the United States, with roughly 450 restaurants in forty-one states. Over four hundred witnesses, most of them current or former employees and nearly half of them white, support charges that African American patrons were denied service, treated poorly, seated in segregated areas, and not allowed to speak with a manager about their complaints.[2]

Cracker Barrel executives vigorously deny the accusations.[3] That matter will be decided in court if a settlement is not negotiated first. But the broad range of the complaints against Cracker Barrel, alleged to have taken place in separate incidents in more than two hundred cities in thirty states, suggests some kind of corporate breakdown in its sensitivity to racial equality.

At least Cracker Barrel (and its customers) can take heart that a dramatic change in corporate practice is possible. Another major U.S. restaurant chain, Denny's, practically reinvented itself.

CHANGING THE MENU AT DENNY'S

The Cracker Barrel grievance is the largest civil rights case against a restaurant corporation since 1994, when Denny's paid out $54 million in two separate race discrimination lawsuits.[4] At the time, Denny's also was charged with failing to serve African Americans; some of its restaurants even obliged blacks to pay a cover charge before they were served. Beyond financial damages, the settlements forced Denny's to train employees in racial sensitivity and feature people of color in advertising in order "to convey to the public that all potential customers, regardless of their race or color, are welcome at Denny's."[5]

Jim Adamson became the CEO of Denny's parent company, Advantica, a year after the company reached a settlement with the U.S. Justice Department. Adamson contends that Denny's was not remarkably racist when he arrived. "I firmly believe that Denny's reflects most Fortune 500 companies where diversity and inclusiveness are a memo as opposed to part of the corporate culture," he says.[6] All the same, one of his first acts as CEO was to replace the entire senior management of the company as well as its board of directors. He also directly oversaw the implementation of an aggressive diversity-training program.[7]

To Adamson's credit, Denny's made great strides. In 1992, only one African American owned a Denny's franchise, and the restaurant chain's national supplier base did not include a single minority contract. Today, sixty-six African Americans are owners of Denny's franchises, and contracts with minority-owned suppliers comprise 18 percent of total corporate purchases.[8]

Its remarkable turnaround has not gone unnoticed: Denny's was honored with the top position in *Fortune* magazine's "best companies for minorities" in 2001.[9] "Denny's got to the table of enlightenment," Adamson says. "I wish more companies did."[10]

Is Your Company Vulnerable to Discrimination?

Companies do not have to treat discrimination as if it were outside their control, like an earthquake or other natural disaster. They can carefully establish procedures for hiring, evaluating, and promoting employees solely on merit. Two people equally qualified deserve the same chance for advancement, and two people doing the same work deserve the same rewards (or lack thereof). In sum, every individual is offered access to the same resources to achieve the mission of the company.

These principles seem basic and straightforward, yet remarkably few corporations manage diversity well. A four-year study focusing on employment practices in large to midsized U.S. corporations shows that more than one in three employers is culpable of discrimination.[11] Conducted by researchers at Rutgers Law School, the study even designated twenty-two thousand American companies as "hard-core discriminators": their hiring of women and minorities was far below comparable companies in their respective industries and geographical locale.

The Rutgers study did not find progressive employment practices even in states with sizable minority populations. In Massachusetts, for example, black workers pursuing a new job, a promotion, a work assignment, or other employment-related activity faced discrimination 40 percent of the time. A Hispanic worker faced a 38 percent probability of discrimination, and women overall 23 percent.

In their final report, the researchers declared, "A substantial part of the public has erroneously assumed that intentional job discrimination is either a thing of the past or the acts of individual 'bad apples' in an otherwise decent work environment. . . . Meanwhile, thousands of employers have continued systematic restriction of qualified minority and female workers."[12]

It is often difficult for people inside a company to recognize their own diversity problems. That blind spot tends to be especially prevalent for workers who are not themselves members of a minority group. For that reason, I found it useful to design a brief diversity inventory that helps to alert a firm to areas that need attention. Apply the inventory that follows to a company with which you have a close association:

- Do employees generally feel that their talents and skills are well rewarded?

- Does the company suffer from a disproportionate level of turnover among women or specific ethnic groups?

- Are there frequent complaints about the fairness of the promotion process?

- Are worker policies and benefits attractive to diverse recruits?

- How much does the company spend annually on recruitment, and how do those figures compare with benchmarks in its industry?

- Do departing workers report not feeling valued, included, or heard?

- If the company's wage scale were broken down by the gender and race in comparable positions, would it show parity?

- What percentage of management positions do women or people of color fill?

- How many women and people of color are on the board of directors?

- How much have discrimination and harassment suits cost the company in the past five years, if both legal fees and settlements are included?

- Is diversity reflected in the company's supplier network?

- How frequently does conflict arise among groups of workers?

Perhaps this inventory unearths a few trouble spots. Taking immediate action to address the root causes could end up saving the company from a lot of pain down the road. Companies with comprehensive diversity programs face less worker conflict, far fewer grievances, and fewer expensive lawsuits.

Half-hearted efforts to hire a few token workers won't do. Building a balanced workforce demands a deep commitment from top to bottom in the organization. So where do you begin? The Charles Schwab Corporation exemplifies a vibrant program for introducing diversity into the corporate culture.

THE POWER OF ONE AT CHARLES SCHWAB

"*Diversity* shouldn't be a code word for hiring more black people," cautions Phyllis Jackson, the straight-shooting vice president of diversity at Charles Schwab.[13] Corporate diversity happens, she claims, when individuals learn to be authentic—comfortable in their own skin—so that they can communicate respectfully and effectively with clients and colleagues regardless of their personal identity.

Does that mean that Phyllis ignores the demographics of Schwab employees? Absolutely not, but she believes in starting where people are at rather than trying to force them to accept a view of the world that does not match their experience. "Given that 70 percent of corporate workers today are white males, we would be foolish to overlook how respecting diversity will improve their own work environment," she asserts.

Besides, she adds, if a corporation does not welcome diversity, altering the makeup of its workforce will not lead to a higher tolerance for difference. She points out that employee retention at Schwab is affected by the degree to which employees feel that equality and dignity are valued and practiced in the day-to-day work environment. Her experience at Schwab is borne out in corporations at large. Research shows that 65 percent of women of color who leave management positions say their companies failed to address gender bias, and 72 percent claim that their companies did not deal effectively with racism.[14] Intrigued by her philosophy of diversity, I asked Phyllis to run me through a workshop she runs for employees at Charles Schwab.

Most of us hang out socially with people who share our background and hold biases toward groups with whom we have limited contact. It is not surprising that this dynamic spills over into work. Colleagues can sit in adjoining cubicles for months and have very little to say to each other, let alone embark on meaningful collaboration on a work project. "We often fear those who are different from us," notes Phyllis. "Fear is based on discomfort, and discomfort is based on inexperience."

For that reason, Phyllis usually starts her diversity workshop with a simulation game. To kick it off by asking people to share honest feelings about workers whom they see every day could turn out to be disastrous. A game, to the contrary, builds a safe environment for later discussion.

Phyllis especially likes the BaFa BaFa game that is popular among cross-cultural trainers. BaFa BaFa was originally designed for use in the U.S. Navy to reduce the number of embarrassing incidents that occur when sailors take shore leave on foreign soil. Essentially, the game simulates the disorientation that travelers typically feel when they visit an unfamiliar culture.

Workshop participants are placed in one of two groups, the Alpha or the Beta culture. The Alpha culture is a warm, friendly society that prizes personal relationships and physical closeness, yet it also has a clear chain of command and respects formal traditions. In the Beta culture, only performance matters: "time is money" and "you are what you earn." To simulate the difficulty of dealing with an alien tongue, the game gives the Beta culture its own trading language. BaFa BaFa in fact means "four" in the Beta language.

Once participants are immersed in the rules, customs, and values of "their" own culture, they pay a visit to the other land. The "travelers" typically feel confused and out of place. Bewilderment can turn to intolerance and hostility once the visitors return home.

Once the simulation game ends, Phyllis asks her colleagues to reflect on their behavior and the judgments they made. She takes it as a healthy sign when groups can stand back and have a good laugh over their inability to understand each other. Participants usually are amazed about the intensity of feeling that a game could evoke.

Phyllis next asks her colleagues to apply the lessons of their simulated experience to Schwab. What assumptions do they make about the people who work at the company? How often do they feel alienated when they visit a department that speaks

---

Creating a Balanced Workforce

A starter kit . . .

- Start where workers are at, not where you want them to be.

- Place them in nonthreatening yet strange environments that require collaboration and personal sharing.

- Highlight the mechanisms they use to cope in a strange environment.

- Ask individuals to identify what they view as "strange cultures" at their workplace.

- Identify the cultural assumptions that inform personal behavior.

- Name the informal divisions that shape actual company policies and operations.

- Devise strategies to connect across the divisions.

another language—perhaps the information technology division, finance, or sales and marketing? If a coworker comes from a different racial, gender, or sexual orientation, at what point does an individual start feeling uncomfortable with the other? Do they consciously or unconsciously avoid uncomfortable relationships? How do these social barriers limit their ability to be productive across silos, departments, and hierarchies at Schwab? This investigation usually yields a long list of social hurdles that people experience at the company. In the final stage of the workshop, Phyllis brainstorms with her colleagues on how to overcome these hurdles.

A Schwab employee who works in the customer service center sent a stirring message to Phyllis after taking one of her diversity workshops. His note indicates that the workshop is helping to create a new mental space at Schwab:

> *This exercise was a true eye-opener to me on the importance of understanding several aspects of diversity. Here are my key learning points:*
>
> 1. *Diversity is not just about skin color, gender, sexual orientation or religious affiliation.*
>
> 2. *The value of a diverse workforce isn't just about intellectual contribution. It's also about reflecting and working to understand the values and communication systems of the people we work for and with.*
>
> 3. *I've known fleetingly what it's like to live in a culture that is totally foreign to me, but I don't know what it's like to have to adapt myself to that culture.*

4. *In the past, I've assumed that to speak with credibility and passion about the value of diversity you had to be considered "diverse"; in other words, the middle-age white male can't be that champion.*

Phyllis, you did a great job [teaching us] that honoring our diverse backgrounds is the responsibility of everyone.

Phyllis reports that she often receives this kind of feedback from her colleagues. Many of them add that the workshops have an impact on their lives beyond work. "Despite differences in religion or skin color or sexual expression, we know intuitively that we're connected to each other," says Phyllis. "To bring down those barriers can be very liberating."

WE ARE MORE THAN COPIES

To nurture an open and tolerant culture is an essential starting point for building a balanced workforce. To move a step further, underrepresented groups need meaningful channels for voicing their concerns and mechanisms for bringing about change. Xerox provides the road map for this next stage of the journey.

In May 1968, racial strife in Rochester, New York, then the corporate home of Xerox, led the company's senior leaders to some serious soul searching.[15] It was one month after the assassination of Martin Luther King Jr., and riots had rocked urban Rochester. C. Peter McColough, then president of Xerox, addressed a memo to all his managers:

We, like all Americans, share the responsibility for a color-divided nation; and in all honesty, we need not look beyond

*our own doorstep to find out why. . . . In Rochester, one of
the first American cities scarred by racial strife, Xerox continues to employ only a very small percentage of Negroes.
In other major cities, including some that have suffered
even greater violence, we employ no Negroes at all.*

McColough closed his letter imploring Xerox managers around
the country to begin aggressively hiring black employees.[16]

Origins of the Caucus Group

Months later, the firm's African American employees took the
lead in forming regional groups referred to as caucus groups.
Ernest Hicks, one of the first black sales representatives hired
at Xerox, reports that the early caucus groups would gather regularly in employees' homes with a focus on self-improvement.[17]
They might help each other sharpen a business proposal or
become more familiar with equipment that would be used in
presentations to a customer or a manager. "We realized that our
own performance and results would determine the image of
blacks at Xerox and possibly open doors for others to come,"
says Hicks.

The caucus groups also made sure that management never
lost sight of its commitment to offer equal opportunity to all
Xerox workers. Hicks reports that even after Xerox started hiring more black sales representatives, their careers did not often
advance at the same pace as did those of their white counterparts. The local black caucus would take specific cases of bias
to senior management and offer its help in identifying black
candidates who merited advancement. Xerox executives inter-
vened in most instances to resolve the inequity, according
to Hicks.

The regional black caucuses eventually unified to form a national body. Their success within the company spawned the creation of other independent caucus groups to promote the advancement of women, Hispanics, Asians, and gay and lesbian employees. Although all caucus members are Xerox employees, the caucuses form and operate apart from the corporate structure. Caucus meetings take place outside work time. Employees even have to take vacation time to attend regional and national conferences.

The influence of caucuses on Xerox over the years is signaled by the fact that minority groups make up 31 percent of the company's total U.S. workforce today. More impressive still, 37 percent of Xerox senior executives are women or people of color, or both.

An in-depth look at the Hispanic caucus provides some clues as to why the caucus mechanism has been so effective at Xerox.

The Inner Workings of the Caucus

Seven Xerox employees established the Hispanic Association for Professional Advancement (HAPA) in 1977.[18] At the time, there were only three Hispanic managers in Xerox's U.S. operation.

Today, Alicia Fernández-Campfield, Xerox's national billing manager, is one of over 250 Hispanics in managerial positions at the company. Alicia also serves as president of HAPA's national board, which governs a membership of over four thousand Hispanic Xerox workers spread across the United States.

Alicia can offer a seasoned perspective on a balanced workforce. A mechanical engineer by training, she came to Xerox in

1998 following an eight-year stint at another Fortune 500 company. Alicia helped to establish a diversity group at this other firm; a scarcity of minority employees made it impractical to launch more specific identity groups. But her diversity group struggled to gain the kind of leverage that could influence corporate policies, she says.

The combination of inspired caucuses and responsive senior management makes the difference at Xerox, according to Alicia. "The caucuses set the agenda, yet absent a solid commitment from management, our voices wouldn't be heard."

A senior Xerox manager in fact is assigned to be the champion of each caucus for a three-year term. The champions report directly to the CEO and carry the concerns of their respective caucuses to meetings at the highest corporate level. Because Xerox wants its senior managers to see the company through many eyes, the champion is chosen specifically to be of a different origin or background from the caucus group. Alicia believes that this policy benefits the caucus group as well: "We already have Hispanics who are our advocates. Champions with a novel perspective can influence their fellow managers in a way we never could."

HAPA's current champion is Tom Dolan, the head of Xerox's global services. At the beginning of each year, HAPA's leadership team meets with Dolan to set a list of goals and action items. They then meet quarterly to monitor their progress on that list.

HAPA proposed a very direct action item to Dolan at the beginning of 2001. The global services division did not have a single Hispanic on its senior staff. Dolan agreed to look for Hispanic candidates. The manner in which Dolan made his commitment impressed Alicia most of all. "He didn't just say, 'Okay, I'll give it a try.' He put it down in bold ink so that we could inspect him on it." By the end of the year, Dolan hired a Hispanic to a senior vice president position.

HAPA members also gain access to senior managers at their national conference. Xerox's CEO, Anne Mulcahy, often attends the event with her senior staff, meeting informally with HAPA members in workshops and over meals. Mulcahy's presence at a HAPA event is more than window dressing. Alicia claims she has a direct line to the CEO's office, and her queries are met with prompt and substantive responses.

A listening ear is no replacement for effective corporate policy, of course. Under Xerox's balanced workforce strategy, managers are evaluated on their track record for hiring, retaining, and promoting minorities and women. Caucuses ensure that fairness is practiced consistently throughout the organization. Their antennas are attuned especially during periods of high layoffs, as in 2001, when Xerox was forced to reduce its total U.S. workforce by nearly 10 percent.

At the time, several HAPA members

Employee Caucuses at Xerox Are More Than Talk

Caucuses offer minority employees . . .

○ A sense of belonging and community

○ Self-improvement tools to enhance work performance

○ Role models and guides

○ An advocate for retention and advancement

○ Increased access to senior management

○ A formal mechanism for addressing unfair corporate practices alerted Alicia that the business unit where they worked was targeted for downsizing; a sizable group of Hispanic workers, ranging from middle managers to clerical positions, would lose their jobs. Alicia and her HAPA colleagues already were concerned about the declining number of Hispanics in the company, so she garnered the names of the workers and sent a list to Dolan with a plea to keep them employed. The business unit was shut down as planned, but most of the Hispanic workers were retained and placed in other Xerox divisions.

The operating principle at Xerox is balance, not favoritism. Management in the above case was sensitive to a disproportionate hit on one segment of its employee base. In the words of Ernest Hicks, the one-time Xerox sales representative who is now the director of corporate diversity, "You don't build inclusion by focusing on only your own group. You have to keep the big picture in mind."[19]

Outside of Xerox, corporate managers might fear that a caucus strategy would lead to a balkanization of the company. A Harvard Business School case study of caucus groups at Xerox contradicts that assumption.[20] It found that when a caucus group raised a complaint, the cause usually could be traced to poor management. In other words, caucuses address problems that affect white workers as well. Many times the communication channels set up by the caucus allowed for more immediate attention and intervention, according to the Harvard study.

For over thirty years, the employee caucuses at Xerox have served as both critics and partners. Above all, it appears, they serve as the firm's conscience.

CASTING A WIDE NET

One of the most blatant cases of employer discrimination I ever personally encountered took place at a technology company, and the bias had nothing to do with race or gender.

The firm's executives had devised a secret code to rate the potential of a job candidate. During an interview, they would casually ask an applicant about his or her personal life. If a candidate divulged that he or she was a parent, the executives feigned interest and asked questions about the ages and hobbies of the children. Proud parents of two children (or more) did not realize that they had been assigned a rating of 4 on a scale of 1 (highest) to 4 (lowest). Candidates with one child pushed their rating down to a 3. Having a spouse or significant other but no children won a score of 2. If the recruit confessed to being single without any attachments, the executives assigned that individual a prime rating of 1.

Although this so-called attachment rating was not the sole factor the executives used in making hiring decisions, it did weigh heavily in their selections. They shared with me their rationale: "We want people here who will give us 150 percent. The more family attachments they have, the more reasons they have to go home at 5:00 P.M. or balk at spending the weekend on a work project." It's a good thing I wasn't pursuing a job with the company; being a father to four children under the age of ten at the time would have blown me off their rating chart.

The leaders of this company demonstrated a terribly narrow view of a worker's potential. Future performance cannot be gauged by the number of hours an employee can be chained to a desk. Experience and training, skills, leadership, integrity, intelligence, creativity, and persistence are surely more valuable assets to look for in a candidate.

A workforce teems with creative energy when people bring to the job a rich variety of experience and background. B&Q, one of the largest retailers in the United Kingdom with three hundred stores and twenty-five thousand employees, can attest to the benefit of casting a wide net.[21]

The British retailer was expanding at an amazing clip in the late 1980s, so much so that its recruitment efforts struggled to keep pace. It underwent a close review of its hiring process and concluded that it was ignoring large segments of the population as potential candidates, especially women who were returning to the workforce after a career break, as well as older adults.

As it was making plans to open a new store in Macclesfield, England, B&Q decided to run a pilot project: it would staff the store entirely with adults over the age of fifty. The retailer was concerned initially that an older workforce would face physical barriers on the job or perhaps would struggle to learn computer systems that were essential for store operations.

These concerns turned out to be unfounded. An independent survey taken two years after the opening of the Macclesfield store found that its staff outperformed other B&Q stores in nearly every meaningful category of job performance: turnover, absenteeism, average sales per worker, and customer satisfaction. Flush with success, B&Q changed its recruiting policies on a corporatewide level to attract and retain mature adult workers better.

Taking its hiring experiment a step further, B&Q next turned its attention to the largely untapped potential of disabled people in the retail sector. Once again, the company set up a pilot program in a single store, completely remodeling its facilities to allow for easy access. And once again, the store's staff turned out impressive results. B&Q expanded the hiring program to all of its stores, working with a national disability group to amend its employee training to take special needs into account.[22]

B&Q has gained strong returns on its hiring programs. Not only does the company get flattering media coverage for its enlightened employment policies, it wins enthusiastic customer support from groups that feel the company cares about who they are. Best of all, B&Q no longer has difficulty finding qualified workers.

LOAN SHARKS AND OTHER PREDATORS

Narrowing the profile of a desirable employee to irrelevant categories like skin color, age, gender, or sexual orientation ultimately hurts the corporation. The fact that employer bias persists nonetheless suggests the dogged resilience of social prejudice.

To profile potential customers along these lines is just as irrational and counterproductive to sound business practice. But it too persists. For decades, banks denied mortgages to entire neighborhoods based on the average income and dominant race of residents.

The civil rights movement pushed for federal laws that now require banks to serve minority and low-income areas. Financial institutions periodically must divulge detailed information about their lending activities and show evidence of serving neighborhoods fairly. By and large, the laws have made a positive impact on lending policies. Blatant redlining, when financial institutions literally draw a red line around entire neighborhoods regarded as off-limits for loans, is rare today.

Discrimination persists in more subtle forms, however. During the late 1990s, a large-scale consolidation of the banking industry in the United States precipitated the massive closure of local bank branches. The first branches to be cut were usually those located in low-income districts. As banks with responsible lending practices moved out, predatory lenders moved in.

Predatory lenders target subprime borrowers, that is, people deemed to be high credit risks. They advertise aggressively in low-income neighborhoods, blanketing the community with fliers and even door-to-door sales calls. But the loans they offer often are designed so that the customer can't keep up with the payments, so that the lender can obtain the property or offer the victim a fresh loan with a new round of fees and expenses.[23] Recent acquisitions of notorious subprime lenders by corporate banks create the real danger that subprime lending might enter mainstream banking.[24]

A study conducted in Oakland, California, shows that subprime lending is one of the primary channels of lending in a minority neighborhood. In Oakland, subprime loans were 36 percent of all refinancing loans made to African American home owners and 17 percent of those made to Latino home owners, but only 9.5 percent of those made to white home owners. The race-based prevalence of subprime loans became even more evident once researchers controlled the data for income levels.[25]

The insurance industry is not as closely monitored on discriminatory practices as banks are—yet, that is. Momentum is building to expand laws on the books for financial institutions to regulate insurance. Community groups and several U.S. state insurance commissions allege that the insurance industry declines to write policies to low-income and minority home owners and charges excessive premiums in targeted neighborhoods.

Regulation is not the only threat on the horizon for the insurance industry. At least a dozen major insurance companies are facing civil lawsuits for widespread race profiling.[26]

Becoming a Good Neighbor, One Block at a Time

Despite the negative trends, some hopeful practices are taking root in the financial industry as well. A number of major banks and insurance companies are working hard to make allies in low-income and minority areas. Safeco is a prime example of a company that takes the time to understand distinct neighborhoods and create the right pathway to develop new markets.

Making New Friends

Safeco is known for insurance, baseball (its name adorns the Seattle Mariners home ballpark), and perhaps little else outside the Seattle area. In urban Seattle, however, the company has built a reputation for a whole lot more. Safeco established in 1999 the Jackson Street Center, a community hub in the heart of Seattle.[27] The center caps a long string of attempts by Safeco to set a footprint in minority and low-income neighborhoods.

The Jackson Street Center's marquee activities take place at its neighborhood academy, which is part adult education school, part quilting bee. Twice a week, it offers seminars at no cost to local residents. Some seminars provide financial advice like managing household budgets and small-scale investing, geared to people hoping to enter the housing market one day. For existing home owners, workshops are offered on do-it-yourself remodeling and refinancing. But more times than not, the academy courses are just plain fun: seminars like planting an organic garden and tips for identifying antiques in your attic. "Home ownership and good neighborliness are prime assets that make a community a great place to live," says Debbie Bird, who directs the Jackson Street Center. "Our academy aims to be a catalyst for making that happen."[28]

Because it offers to local community groups the use of a multipurpose room and a boardroom at no cost, the Jackson Street Center quickly became popular with small businesses and nonprofits as a meeting site. The multipurpose room comes well equipped with a VCR, a white board, flip charts, and a steaming pot of coffee. The rooms are typically booked two to three months out on the calendar, six days a week. The center also provides financial grants to help nonprofits fulfill their mission in the neighborhood; it gave out nearly $100,000 in 2002.[29]

Community Development as Business Development

Safeco does not sell its policies directly to the public; it relies on independent sales agents to serve as its distributors. An insurance agent who licenses Safeco's products typically sells a range of products from other insurance companies as well. As part of its urban business strategy, Safeco is recruiting independent agents who are more diverse.

In 2001, Safeco opened its second urban center in Atlanta and is looking at expanding to a third city in the near future. Safeco's director of community relations, Rose Lincoln, admits that the company struggles internally to balance the importance of investing in diversity against immediate profitability. "Because the return on investment is not immediate in our neighborhood work, it is a challenge to convince bottom-line-oriented managers that we're not talking about pure philanthropy here, but community investment."[30]

Lincoln stresses that people consistently say in marketing surveys that they want to buy insurance from people who have lived their cultural experience. Given that the insurance industry at large can boast very few agents who are women or minorities, many customers may not feel sufficient levels of trust to buy a policy, she adds.

The Jackson Street Center set a goal to recruit and train ten new agents for urban Seattle in 2002. If they all turn out like Michael Wong, the company will be ecstatic.

Michael, age forty, was born and raised in south-central Seattle.[31] For nearly ten years, he labored to build a career selling insurance, moving between several major insurance firms as an in-house sales agent. He dreamed of running his own business one day, but had doubts that it was actually possible.

It usually takes at least five years to build a client base of first-time customers and renewals that could bring a new insurance agent a livable wage. That fact makes recruiting sales agents in minority and low-income neighborhoods especially difficult.

Michael believed that the Jackson Street Center offered him his best shot at becoming an independent agent. Safeco put him through a training program, set him up in an office with a computer, and put a network of seasoned underwriters at his disposal should he run into any complex problems. Most important of all, the center fed him strong potential leads. And it didn't hurt to have a few Seattle Mariners tickets to give out to some of his new business clients.

Michael kept his office at the center for two and a half years before moving out and hanging up his own shingle. He continues to build on the partner-

---

Five Essential Steps for Diversifying Your Customer Base

1. Establish a physical presence in communities where you are underrepresented.

2. Develop strong links with local civic groups.

3. Provide resources that strengthen the neighborhood.

4. Recruit sales representatives from the community.

5. Tailor products and services to meet local needs.

---

ships with Asian cultural groups and other organizations he met while he was at the center. "The insurance business is all about trust," says Michael, "so the center's commitment to the neighborhood generates a lot of positive feelings that I can build on."

A Colorful Supply Chain

As the Safeco experience shows, diversity cannot be reduced to political correctness. Many corporations view it as a business opportunity. A firm that invests in a balanced workforce is more likely to reflect its customer base.

That's clearly the attitude at SBC Communications, the San Antonio–based telephone company that holds the overall brand for Ameritech, Nevada Bell, Pacific Bell, Southwestern Bell, and Southern New England Telephone. "We do not necessarily aim to mirror the nation's labor force, but the population we serve," declares Margaret Makihara Cerrudo, SBC's senior vice president of human resources.[32] The numbers bear her out: nearly 35 percent of SBC's customers are people of color, and its employees are 38 percent people of color and 48 percent female.[33]

A research study measuring the factors that influence minority consumer choice of a long-distance telephone service provider validates the wisdom of SBC's diversity strategy. Sponsored by the Lucent Corporation, the study found that minorities pay close attention to whether a provider creates jobs and income for their racial group. It was the third most important factor, after price and quality, that influences their choice of provider.[34]

In addition to its balanced workforce, a big asset, SBC's supplier diversity program further enhances its competitive edge in minority communities. Minority entrepreneurs often identify lucrative niche opportunities long before mainstream companies make those discoveries. Alliances with minority suppliers can help as well to avoid costly mistakes when a company expands into a minority market. But above all, to build a diverse supplier base increases the pool of intellectual capital that a corporation can tap.

The extraordinary relationship that exists between SBC and one of its suppliers, the Telamon Corporation, exemplifies the potential.

Customizing the Network

When AT&T was forced into divestiture in 1984, Albert Chen, at the time a thirteen-year veteran of the telecommunications industry, saw a market space open up for a specialized integrator of telecom systems. In 1984, he founded Telamon to fill the gap.[35] Albert's insight was justified. Telamon, based in Indianapolis, grew steadily and reached close to $15 million in annual revenues by 1992.

That was also the year Albert heard about SBC's aggressive recruitment of minority-owned suppliers. He called SBC's procurement group and made an immediate impression. SBC was looking to speed up the process of customizing the network hardware that it was buying from manufacturers, and the Asian-owned supplier offered the right solution. In short order, SBC introduced Albert to four of its principal equipment manufacturers, including Nortel Networks.

Nortel made Telamon one of its preferred partners to configure and service its hardware for SBC networks. Being selected to sit between Nortel and SBC was an important win for Telamon, and it meant that his company had to push its performance into a higher gear. During the developmental phase of the new project, both Nortel and SBC provided Telamon employees with extensive training in product manufacturing, quality control, and order processing. "A disadvantaged business usually struggles in two essential areas, management skills and financial stability," shares Albert, then adds, "SBC gives Telamon assistance in both."

SBC has an alliance in place with four highly regarded U.S. business schools—the Kellogg School of Northwestern University, UCLA's Anderson School of Business, the Tuck School of Dartmouth College, and the University of Texas at San Antonio—to offer an executive management program to its supplier network. The curriculum at each school makes ample use of real-life case studies aimed to help minority- and women-owned enterprises to break the so-called five-year jinx that pulls 80 percent of all new businesses into failure.[36]

SBC gives generous scholarships to help the companies meet the tuition for their key managers. Albert has sent ten of his own managers to participate. "We can't compete with large companies that have their own corporate management programs," he notes.

SBC conducted $300 million in business with Telamon in 2001, helping to put Albert's company on a remarkable growth path. Its total annual revenues now top $460 million, which means that SBC accounts for 65 percent of the supplier's business. For six consecutive years, Telamon made *INC* magazine's list of fastest-growing private companies in the United States.

SBC's investment has paid off big dividends for its own operations as well. Prior to its business relationship with Telamon, the telecom giant had a waiting period of six to eight weeks on new orders of a particularly important piece of network equipment. Telamon shortened the delivery time down to two to three days. Deployment speed is critical in the telecom industry; when it comes to networking, time really is money.

Understandably, Albert would like to become less reliant on a single client. His goal is to reduce SBC's slice of the company's total sales to 35 percent. SBC once again has stepped up to provide assistance. Its procurement managers have introduced Telamon to other companies that could benefit from its services. Cingular Wireless, a joint venture of SBC and Bell South that operates as an independent corporation, has become a Telamon client in large part due to SBC's enthusiastic endorsement of its track record.

The Message Is Giving Back as Well

SBC's commitment to diversity has made its imprint on Albert's own company. Telamon has works diligently to maintain a balanced workforce: 22 percent of its workers are Hispanic, 16 percent black, and 22 percent Asian. In addition, it follows SBC's supplier model, making 13.5 percent of its own outside purchases with minority- and women-owned businesses. Telamon also mentors two other minority-owned suppliers that are just getting off the ground. Albert and company share freely with them the blueprint for Telamon's own internal operations, such as its quality control systems. This intellectual capital saves the start-up companies from the expensive process of building their own protocols.

"SBC's stance in the marketplace has influenced profoundly our own business philosophy," Albert openly acknowledges. "The message is that you can't just keep taking. You have to give back as well."

The ethos of giving back also may be the only thing that will make globalization work. The next chapter travels from Bangladesh to Canada to Nigeria to Italy in search of the best practices in international trade and commerce.

Chapter Eight

Globalization

Principle Eight

A company will pursue international trade and production based on respect for the rights of workers and citizens of trade partner nations.

Vital Signs

Is corporate policy designed to protect human rights? Does the company promote consistent standards for worker health and safety? Are employees paid a livable wage? Is the free association of workers respected? Are investments initiated or maintained in countries where there is a pattern of ongoing and systemic violation of human rights? Are programs in place to transfer skills and infrastructure in underdeveloped markets where the company operates? Is a dialogue with local communities established to ensure that the project fits into the sustainable development of the region? Are the practices of the company's supplier network monitored and reported openly?

Does the company, or its subcontractors, use children in the production process? Does the company undermine the democratic process in countries where it operates? Are civic institutions strengthened? Are all payments made to public officials publicly reported? Are relationships with foreign entities audited on a regular basis to ascertain if bribes have been made in the procurement or implementation of contracts? Are workers given the tools to identify and report a conflict of interest when it arises?

In 1995, the ruling military junta of Nigeria arrested Ken Saro-Wiwa, an internationally acclaimed author, along with eight other tribal Ogoni people. Following a show trial, the junta executed all nine.

While incarcerated prior to his execution, Saro-Wiwa appealed to the international community "to prevail on the Nigerian government and Shell to stop this carnage, this genocide." For thirty years, a Nigerian oil consortium made up of transnational corporations had run the Ogoni oil fields, pumping out nearly 2 million barrels of oil per day.[1]

At the time, the Shell Oil Corporation owned a 30 percent stake in the consortium. The official Shell response to the execution of the Ogoni Nine was complete silence. The oil firm's position was consistent with its pledge of noninterference in South Africa during the 1980s as the walls of apartheid began to crack. A private firm should not interfere in the domestic politics of countries where it operates, Shell officials argued in its defense. A number of credible human rights groups rebut that Shell was anything but hands-off local politics in Africa.

Be it reality or perception, corporations are viewed as playing a critical role in the social and political affairs of a society. Hence, when firms conduct business as usual in countries with a poor human rights record, they set themselves up for local reprisals and damage to their international reputation. A sizable group of consumers still refuse to this day to buy Shell gasoline, in part due to the corporation's actions, or lack of action, in Nigeria and South Africa.

Transnational corporations are faced with highly complex dilemmas for which there are no simple solutions. The concept of human rights encompasses a broad canopy of concerns that stretch from the treatment of workers to fair trading practices to social and economic development. Yet no matter how distant its supply chain may be, the higher a company's profile is, the further its obligations seem to stretch.

Not All That Glitters Is Gold

The experience of a Canadian mining company, Placer Dome, in South America illustrates the challenges of doing business in a highly uncertain investment climate with a mixed bag of stakeholder expectations. Placer Dome, the third largest gold producer in North America, entered into a joint venture agreement in 1991 with a state-owned enterprise with responsibility for mining development in Venezuela. Placer Dome claimed a 95 percent stake in the venture. The plan was to explore and implement a large-scale commercial development at the Las Cristinas mine, which Placer Dome believed had the potential to yield over 11 million ounces of gold deposits.[2]

The Venezuelan government's decision to grant a mining concession to Placer Dome generated immediate controversy.

The contract essentially displaced local independent miners who had operated in the concession area for a long time. The government defended the deal, arguing that an influx of new jobs and substantial economic development would lead to tangible benefits for the people of the region. Placer Dome in fact had projected a $500 million investment in the project. Those promises did little to calm the anxieties of local miners, who would join an already large unemployed pool in the surrounding region.

Keith Ferguson, the vice president for sustainability at Placer Dome, shares that his company has learned from experience to find common ground with local groups from the start of a project. "It's not simply a matter of imposing our plans," he explains. "We need to show communities how our project fits into the sustainable development of their region."[3]

Ferguson points to a recent round of discussions Placer Dome carried out with native tribes in northern Canada. Many of the tribe's elders did not want a mine developed on their land, but they conceded that younger tribal people were keen to bring in jobs and stimulate economic activity. Before accepting Placer Dome's proposal, the elders wanted a clear idea of what they might expect. Placer Dome took photographs of the land, superimposed a set of images showing how the affected area would look once mining operations commenced, then superimposed a second set of images showing how the land would look after reclamation. The elders were more comfortable with the proposal once they understood the time line toward reclamation.

As Placer Dome discovered in Las Cristinas, however, events do not always unfold as planned. Falling gold prices on the international markets put the project on hold. By February

2001, the price of gold had declined to almost $100 per ounce below the minimum target price Placer Dome had determined would make the project financially viable.

The repeated postponement of a starting date for mining operations aggravated social tensions in the region. When another in a series of suspensions was announced in mid-1999, a delegation of miners and community leaders led a march to the Las Cristinas camp gate. They demanded that Placer Dome grant a concession for small-scale artisans to resume their mining on the property. If the corporation did not comply with their demands, they declared, disruptive actions and a negative press campaign would ensue.

Placer Dome did not want its reputation as a good neighbor tainted. The company regularly negotiates mining concessions with governments around the world, and being perceived as a poor corporate citizen might put it at a distinct disadvantage in future negotiations. The mining company also hoped to maintain goodwill in the Las Cristinas region in case rising gold prices made it feasible to initiate large-scale mining.

Placer Dome therefore committed itself to work with community groups on two significant development projects. The first project was designed to help small-scale miners earn a living. Under the terms of a negotiated agreement, four newly formed miners' associations were permitted to mine in the concession area under company supervision. Placer Dome also provided technical training to the miners and monitored the environmental impact of their operations.

The second project focused on bringing a community-based health care system to the region. The rural areas surrounding the Las Cristinas mine had extremely limited access to health care. No local clinic, for example, had the capacity to take X-rays, do laboratory analysis, or conduct major surgeries. In addition to addressing this scarcity in direct health care, the project made it a priority to establish systems for adequate sewage and waste collection in sur-rounding communities.

Local leaders un-derstood the risks of

Win-Win-Win

Social investments aim to satisfy a number of partners:

- The local business unit earns a social license to operate, thereby reducing the risk of civil actions, shutdowns, and negative publicity.

- Local community groups gain an improved standard of living and a positive partnership with the business venture.

- The corporation strengthens its reputation as an operator of choice, a status useful in winning the rights to operate in other regions.

---

building a health care system on the largesse of a single financial benefactor, and the uncertainty of the Las Cristinas mining operation heightened their concerns. Project leaders therefore brought together a coalition of eighteen groups, including Placer Dome, governmental agencies, and international aid groups. In this way, they were able to leverage Placer Dome's investment of $500,000 into a capital pool of more than $2 million. Maybe even more remarkable, the crowded room of devel-opment partners did not slow the project's progress. The health center opened its doors in February 2001.

It would be nice to end the story there with a tidy ending, but subsequent events have led to a more uncertain future. Placer Dome finally abandoned its plans at Las Cristinas in July 2001. The government of Venezuela felt betrayed by the withdrawal and lashed out publicly against the Canadian conglomerate. Placer Dome defends itself, saying it acted in good faith in Las Cristinas and should not be blamed for a plummeting gold market. Local miner associations continue to push forward their interests, now in dialogue with the new proprietors of the mines.

There are no villains in the Las Cristinas story; if anything, the case illustrates the tough road of economic development in impoverished regions. The critics of globalization depict transnational corporations as carnivores, ever ready to prey on the weak and vulnerable. If the business enterprise is to make a convincing retort, it will come from the transfer of skills and infrastructure that makes tangible social improvement a reality. A successful venture in Bangladesh, made possible only by significant foreign investment and intellectual capital, points to such an inclusive practice of capitalism.

CREATING WEALTH AT THE BOTTOM OF THE PYRAMID

The vision for GrameenPhone, the telephone company with the largest subscriber base on the Indian subcontinent, ironically arose from technical failure. On an otherwise normal afternoon in New York City in 1993, investment banker Iqbal Quadir's computer network went down.[4]

The frustration of an unproductive day jogged a childhood memory in his native Bangladesh. When Iqbal was eleven years old, his mother one day had implored him to fetch medicine from a neighboring town. It took Iqbal half a day to walk the seven or so miles to the village, only to discover that the medicine man was not there. He made the long trek back home in despair.

Years later, sitting idle in his New York investment firm, Iqbal reflected on how much more productive he and his neighbors in Bangladesh would have been with even the most basic communication device. Over 100 million people live in rural Bangladesh without telephones. High demand, low supply—Iqbal mulled the conditions over in his mind, and a business idea was born.

Even brilliant ideas require execution, and Iqbal knew it would not be easy convincing investors that a cellular phone company servicing the poor of Bangladesh would ring up profits. At least he had four years to gather the necessary funds. That's how long it took him to push his way through a labyrinth of governmental regulation to win a mobile phone license in Bangladesh.

Turning Negatives into Market Potentials

In his pitch to investors, Iqbal turned Bangladesh's apparent negatives into market potentials. For example, how do you overcome a virtually nonexistent telecom infrastructure in Bangladesh? At least a new phone company would not have to worry about saturating the market, says Iqbal, quickly reversing field.

The next negative is Bangladesh's arid, flat terrain and dense population, attributes long held to be detriments to economic development in the country. No problem, Iqbal exclaims; these conditions drive down the cost of capital expenditures on infrastructure like transmitting towers.

Granting Iqbal that he is right, there remains one enormous hurdle: Who would want to risk venture capital in an impoverished country like Bangladesh? Only the few and the brave, Iqbal admits, but that would give a well-funded enterprise competitive advantage. Stiff competition from foreign mobile operators would be unlikely.

Iqbal eventually persuaded an unusual consortium of investors to back his venture, anchored by a Scandinavian telephone company and a Bangladeshi bank. Norway's Telenor provided 51 percent of the total start-up investment of $52 million. The Bangladeshi Grameen Bank contributed less financial capital, yet the value of its customer relationships and highly regarded brand was as good as gold. The bank's credibility in fact helped Iqbal win a license from the government to operate a cellular network.

The Grameen Bank is a remarkable story in its own right. The bank opened in 1976 as a way to help people earn their way out of poverty. Its founder, Muhammad Yunus, initially used twenty-six dollars of his own money to make an experimental loan to a group of people who leveraged the funds to make chairs and pots. When the loan was repaid promptly, he made a second loan, and then another. The bank mushroomed, and today it operates in roughly twelve hundred branches, giving out small loans in the range of $100 to $200 to over 2 million customers. Most of the recipients are women, and more than 95 percent of the time they repay their loans.

Grameen Bank got excited about Iqbal's venture once it realized that the venture could promote self-employment, just as the bank itself does. Typically, a Bangladeshi woman comes to Grameen Bank to borrow $100 to buy, say, a cow. The cow produces milk, the woman sells the milk in the local market, and the woman pays back her loan to the bank. Iqbal depicted the cellular phone as a similar kind of cash cow for a local entrepreneur while bringing connectivity to the entire village.

The concept took hold, and Grameen Bank adopted Iqbal's new company as its branded telephone company. They launched a joint marketing plan called Village Phone that gives individuals small, no-collateral loans for cell phones and a 50 percent discount on airtime. The entrepreneurs then turn around and charge customers the market rate for initiating calls. Grameen Bank processes all of the applications and gives loan approval to clients with established credit records.

In the urban areas of Bangladesh, GrameenPhone offers more conventional single-usage service plans, much as Sprint does in the American market. But while growth in the United States and European cellular markets has slowed considerably, GrameenPhone has climbed rapidly to 700,000 paid subscribers.

All the same, the marquee spot belongs to the Village Phone program. Over seventeen thousand people today are self-employed retailers of telephone services. Each telephone yields a monthly usage of $250, about a dozen times the usage of a typical urban subscriber. A telephone generates on average $2 per day after costs, meaning that entrepreneurs bring in

Banking on the Poor

GrameenPhone achieves profitability offering services that . . .

○ Don't require end users to purchase more service than they need.

○ Are in high demand but short supply.

○ Achieve economies of scale by aggregating the needs of many small users.

○ Provide upfront capital and sustainable income for inspired entrepreneurs.

○ Create greater efficiency in relationships.

○ Establish a communications link that stimulates further economic activity.

about $700 annual income, more than double the per capita income in Bangladesh.

Connectivity stimulates productivity in the lives of the rural poor in indirect ways as well. A Village Phone provides a communication link to nearly fifteen hundred people. "In terms of contingent access—if a person needs to make a call, he or she has the means to do so—we have opened a channel to 25 to 30 million people already," Iqbal notes enthusiastically.

Truly, contingent access is a value in itself. Farmers sending bananas to be sold in the city, for example, can find out directly the price for their goods in a city market. Traditionally, middlemen have taken advantage of a discrepancy of information between the urban markets and the rural supplier. Access to communication leads to efficiency, meaning that more money flows back to the farmer and more funds are invested in banana cultivation. "That is authentic rural development," declares Iqbal.

Not only has GrameenPhone proven itself to be an innovative development project in an underdeveloped market, it also has made a good profit. How many start-ups would love to gain $27 million in pretax profits after only five years in business? GrameenPhone achieved that result in 2001, and the company was operating at an even more profitable clip in 2002.

Iqbal no longer plays an operational role in Grameen-Phone. He remains a shareholder in the company, but admits he's more inspired to plant businesses than cultivate them. He now looks to replicate the GrameenPhone model in Uganda or Afghanistan. Although global investments in telecom projects have slowed to a trickle, he believes GrameenPhone's results should make it easier to raise capital this time. Another trend in his favor, he points out, is that the cost of telecom equipment is declining significantly.

There he goes again, turning negatives into market potentials.

Profit Is a Means

"Profit is a means, not an end," declared business professor Russell Ackoff to a classroom full of business students. Profits are necessary to attract equity capital, of course, just as revenues are necessary to pay salaries to employees. But a business enterprise without a clear mission lacks a reason for being, emphasized Ackoff.

Sitting in attendance at the Wharton School in the early 1990s, Iqbal heard Ackoff's message and became an instant believer. "For any given project, the need for capital, the need for electricity, the need for labor should not drive me as an entrepreneur," Iqbal elaborates. "I should be driven by my own vision of what I am trying to create and see everything else as components that require assembly."

Part of his motivation behind launching GrameenPhone was to demonstrate that business can solve real human problems. Developing countries expect too much from the public sector, he argues. Where there is a social problem, the citizens look for the government to solve it. Too much power is acceded to political leaders as a result, a condition that increases the likelihood of corruption.

Put another way, the private sector is so weak in the developing world that there is no countervailing force to balance governmental authority. Iqbal today imparts this message to his own students at Harvard's Kennedy School of Government. He is convinced that until a thriving private sector emerges, developing countries will struggle to improve their governance, itself an important prerequisite for economic progress.

Economic progress and quality of governance have evolved together in most developed countries. Yet Iqbal senses that most citizens of wealthy nations underestimate the role that business has played in creating a stable society: "Because of the scandalous behavior of corporations, people conclude that business creates problems and governments fix them." Business leaders can only blame themselves for this skewed perspective, he adds. Seduced by wealth, they cease to think of profit as a means and view it as an end unto itself.

Most disappointing of all, errant corporate behavior sends the wrong message to the developing world. The United States has succeeded in selling hamburgers, pop music,

Making the Right Call

Iqbal Qadir nails down five planks for an economic development platform:

1. Entrepreneurial energy is a potent force for uplifting impoverished economies.

2. A genuine business survives only by meeting a genuine social need; therefore, economic development and business development must proceed together.

3. Development must find ways to help people connect with each other; connectivity leads to productivity.

4. Digital technologies have the potential to unleash new thinking and create new business models in poor countries. The constant reduction in their costs enhances their applicability to impoverished economies.

5. Appropriate technology is not the key issue. Poor economies need appropriate institutions that can deliver technology so that common people can harness its power for themselves.

and soft drinks globally, but it fails to export values like hard work, integrity, and fair play. "There's something amiss, and I think corporate America can take much of the responsibility," he declares. "Globalization is not about just opening up another Pizza Hut. It means distributing opportunity and the good life to all of the world's population."

THE OPEN-HAND POLICY

The economic potential of the aspiring poor, many of whom look to join the market economy for the first time, is greatly underestimated. Establishing favorable conditions for microenterprise ought to a high priority for any party seriously engaged in long-term social development. All the same, transnational corporations will continue to dominate developing markets for decades to come. How they go about their business therefore is no small matter.

Transparency International (TI), a nongovernmental watchdog that monitors business corruption around the globe, claims that transnational corporations apply a double standard when they operate in developing countries: condemning local corruption while paying bribes to win influence and business contracts in those very markets.

TI publishes an annual Bribe Payers Index based on surveys conducted in developing nations. Its 2002 index shows a high incidence of bribery even when laws are in place that criminalize such behavior. U.S. corporations, for instance, are subject to the Foreign Corrupt Practices Act, yet the TI index shows that American firms are just as prone to use bribes to win business in developing countries as are their German counterparts, which do not risk criminal prosecution for bribery and can even write off payments to foreign officials as a deduction against their income taxes.[5]

Anyone who has operated for any length of time in the developing world may be convinced that payoffs are impossible to avoid. At times, it feels as if the system does not move until you throw a coin into the slot. "You have to play the game" is an opinion I have heard voiced repeatedly.

I know firsthand how complicated the matter of bribes can be. Working in El Salvador, I one day visited the telephone company to order service for our office. I was dismayed to learn that it would take up to six months to get our telephones installed. The agent behind the desk then informed me that he could cut that delay down to two weeks if I greased the right palms, starting with his own, of course. I told him I would wait. The telephones were in fact installed unexpectedly two months later.

U.S. law tries to strike a middle ground on payoffs to foreign officials. The Foreign Corrupt Practices Act permits facilitating payments: small gifts made to obtain low-level approvals or actions, including securing permits and clearing goods through customs. Under these terms, the Salvadoran agent who offered to speed up my telephone installation for a fistful of dollars was looking for a facilitating payment.

U.S. companies are prohibited from making financial payments to foreign officials that would influence a contractual arrangement or give unfair advantage. Such behavior is considered bribery and is a punishable offense.

Although these lines may appear boldly drawn, they can blur quickly in societies where private and public governance wane. It is quite instructive, then, to study how a corporation

Bribe Payers Index

Business experts in fifteen leading underdeveloped countries were
asked, "In the business sectors with which you are most familiar,
please indicate how likely companies from the following countries are to pay or offer bribes to win or retain business in your
country." A perfect score, indicating no perceived propensity to
pay bribes, is 10.

Country Rank	Score
Australia	8.5
Sweden	8.4
Switzerland	8.4
Austria	8.2
Canada	8.1
Netherlands	7.8
Belgium	7.8
United Kingdom	6.9
Singapore	6.3
Germany	6.3
Spain	5.8
France	5.5
United States	5.3
Japan	5.3
Malaysia	4.3
Hong Kong	4.3
Italy	4.1
South Korea	3.9
Taiwan	3.8
People's Republic of China	3.5

Source: Transparency International, *Transparency International Bribe Payers
Index 2002* (Berlin, Germany: Transparency International, 2002).

operating in a number of international markets shapes its policies on corruption. BP, the world's third largest independent oil group, will serve as our model. The U.K.-based energy giant has gone further than any other transnational corporation toward adopting a global standard that takes the needs of underdeveloped societies into account.

OVER-THE-TABLE BUSINESS

Offshore Angola is blessed with some of the most plentiful oil reserves in the world. To date, the African country has commercialized those resources quite successfully. The oil sector provides between 80 and 90 percent of the state's income, worth an estimated $5 billion annually. Sadly, as much as one-third of that income disappears.[6]

Global Witness, a nongovernmental group based in the United Kingdom, claims the money is being siphoned off by corruption. In two separate investigative reports, Global Witness documents how the Angolan government's legitimate exercise of self-defense against militant rebels (UNITA) has turned into a conspiracy to rob the citizenry of its new-found wealth.[7] Politicians and military leaders at the highest levels are implicated in kickback schemes and overpriced arms deals, typically financed by oil-backed loans.

The absence of financial transparency in Angola enables the cash diversion schemes to flourish. The refusal of international oil companies to disclose publicly the payments they make to the Angolan government makes them complicit in this rampant corruption, Global Witness argues. Ordinary Angolan citizens do not have the information they need to call their government to account over the management of income earned from resources that the state is meant to hold in trust for the general population. In effect, oil companies endorse a standard of behavior that would be unacceptable in the nations where they have a home base.[8]

Embracing Transparency

In February 2001, BP broke rank with the other transnational oil companies operating in Angola. In a letter to Global Witness, BP declared its willingness to publish details of its annual oil production in Angola and all payments it makes to the state in exchange for operating in the country.[9] Lord John Browne, BP's chief executive, believes his firm's decision simply makes sound business sense: "The flow of revenue we were providing wasn't clearly traceable by all relative elements of civil society, and that situation put the long-term viability of our project in Angola at risk."[10]

Browne claims that BP has an interest in the long-term health of the societies where it operates. He points out that his company will invest roughly $7 billion in exploration and development in Angola over the next decade and will look for a rate of return on that investment for at least an additional fifteen years. If it finds additional oil reserves along the way, BP may still be operating in Angola in thirty years, which would equal the life span of its stay in both the North Sea and Alaska.

Social critics often assail transnational oil companies for supporting dictatorships in developing countries. Here's the classic scenario: oil companies overlook corruption and blatant violations of human rights, while rogue authorities clear the road of any obstacles for their business interests. Although not discounting that oil companies in the past may have taken this tact, Browne believes the approach backfires. "At some point the dam will burst and the companies who have been party to the authoritarian regime get swept up in the tide," he says, and then adds, "We want to work in societies that are stable and progressive."

A corporation's international reputation will take a damaging hit when the dam bursts as well. Because it services 14 million customers a day globally, BP guards its brand quite closely. "Our brand is dependent on our weakest performance, wherever we operate in the world," declares Browne.

BP's policy on transparency in foreign markets is still relatively new. Given that the company forecasts its growth markets in places like Colombia, China, West Africa, and the Caspian region, that task will not be easy. The oil giant wrestles to develop global standards to fit complex political environments.

Consider foreign business partners: they do not always welcome transparency with a warm embrace. When BP announced that it had paid $111 million as part of a licensing fee to gain the rights to operate in Angola, for example, the company drew fiery criticism from the state-owned oil group, Sonangol. Already under investigation by the International Monetary Fund (IMF) amid the disappearance of more than $1 billion of oil revenues, Sonangol appeared terrified by BP's public disclosure.[11]

Global Witness suggests that such local resistance discourages other oil companies from following BP's example:

BP's experience with Sonangol shows that even if an oil company wants to be transparent it may be threatened with having its concessions terminated and re-assigned to less scrupulous competitors. Despite high-sounding principles, adherence to the bottom line of profits without principles has, so far, ensured that standards of disclosure and transparency in Angola remain those of the lowest common denominator. Oil companies acting collectively could break this deadlock—and send a powerful message about global good governance—but, so far, the industry has lacked the collective imagination to address this problem.[12]

In the past, BP did not prohibit its employees from making facilitation payments. But in early 2002, it changed its policy to ban all facilitation payments made directly or indirectly by any

---

Putting Everything on the Table: Five Steps Toward Full Transparency

1. Publicly report the payments (including taxes) made to national governments in all countries where the firm operates.

2. Provide information about the payments made in the parent company's consolidated annual reports and in annual returns to investment authorities.

3. Provide the same information locally in the national language of each country of operation, as well as in the home language of the company.

4. Embrace a unified stand on full transparency among all companies in the industry sector operating in the country.

5. Adopt a policy of independent, transparent auditing of social programs, disclosing the purpose of projects and their economic value.

Source: Adapted from Global Witness, *All the President's Men: The Devastating Story of Oil and Banking in Angola's Privatised War* (London: Global Witness, 2002), pp. 2–4.

of its business units worldwide. The U.K. oil giant announced at the same time that it would halt all political contributions from its corporate coffers. "We must be particularly careful about the political process, not because it is unimportant, but quite the reverse, because the legitimacy of that process is crucial both for society and for us as a company working in that society," Browne contends.

The rise of globalization is rewriting social expectations. In many places in the world, transnational corporations are being asked to take responsibility for civil society. Corporations cannot be in the business of jurisdiction, of course, but they are being called on to support an economic base and democratic process, both essential platforms for social improvement.

Relationship Mapping

No set of rules can cover every contingency that may arise in the course of doing business internationally. BP's corporate strategy on transparency therefore relies on its own internal democratic process as much as policy.

Wherever BP works, its managers are asked to identify the key social and political relationships that might influence business operation. Individual managers are then assigned to be "owners" of each respective relationship. Key relationships are monitored on an ongoing basis, and the respective owners share relevant information with colleagues as needed. This practice, which BP calls relationship mapping, brings structure and quality assurance to an area of business life that has fallen into an ambiguous world of informal personal networks.

Relationship mapping is not fail-safe, of course. It's effective only to the degree that managers fully report any state of affairs that might compromise their judgment or action. Conflicts of interest, real or perceived, raise doubts about the company's integrity. BP therefore strongly urges its employees never to put themselves or their colleagues in a position where their loyalties are divided.

If employees harbor any doubts, they are instructed to report their concern to a superior. Any conflict, real or perceived, then passes through an evaluation process. Hot-line

Scouting for Red Flags

To help workers identify a conflict of interest when it arises, BP has designed a short self-evaluation tool for its workers in the field:

○ Do you feel comfortable dealing with this person or company given your relationship with either?

○ Would you be concerned if everyone knew what the relationship was and you remained involved in the business transaction, especially if a deal was concluded?

○ Would people think you assisted this individual or company preferentially to get business?

○ Do you feel under any obligation due to the relationship you have?

○ Would you feel embarrassed or awkward if they do not obtain the business and you have been involved?

○ Do you feel unduly influenced to make this person or this company successful in the business?

○ Do you stand to gain anything (reputation, value, money) by virtue of your relationship with the individual?

Source: BP corporate document, n.d.

telephone numbers and e-mail provide employees with an easy and effective way of reporting, anonymously if need be, possible violations of law or company policy. BP managers, in turn, are expected to report to the company's investigation and fraud center serious violations, breaches of ethical conduct, fraud, or other criminal acts.

"The larger and more complex the company, the more challenging transparency becomes," admits Browne. "We believe the best strategy is to acknowledge that we have processes in place to manage these relationships and describe them openly."

SWEATING THE DETAILS

Globalization once was held up as a dream for lifting the world's poor. So far that dream has not materialized, but it's not too late for globalization to work. To a great extent, its destiny lies in the hands of global corporations: Will they practice equitable rules to benefit ordinary citizens wherever they operate in the globe?

Forms of Diminished Opportunity

The naysayers of globalization are quick to conjure up the image of a sweatshop. My own experience confirms that the image is not an illusion. Its meaning is less clear.

I recall my first business start-up. The venture capitalist looked me straight in the eyes and uttered the words that every hungry entrepreneur wants to hear: "I can offer your company a real competitive edge." My partners and I were searching for seed capital to launch our technology company. But we also needed talent—a network of experienced workers who would help us to execute our business plan successfully—so we were keen to learn how this particular investor was going to give us the vaunted competitive edge.

"I run a sweatshop with more than three hundred software engineers in Shanghai," he explained, absent any remorse at his choice of words, let alone his business practice. "We pay them a fraction of what we'd pay to build a technology system here in the United States," he added.

At least the investor was honest, but his choice of words caused me to run the other way. If he had told me that he had a "low-cost labor force" in China, I would have been more open to exploring his offer. Most antiglobalization activists would probably think that I'm just playing a game of semantics, but the distinction matters. Wage parity for workers on a global scale is not in the cards, nor would it necessarily help poor countries if it were. Antiglobalization movements need to consider whether some of their positions, if implemented, might actually diminish the choices of people from developing nations.

Sweatshop to me implies a specific form of diminished opportunity. Sweatshops do not guarantee a living wage or other basic rights that respect the dignity of workers. Our social goals to create wealth should coincide with our ideals of human development. The process is a virtuous circle. Work is sanctified by its contribution to the well-being of others, especially the less fortunate, and the fulfillment of workers increases the wealth of all. The fact that some major corporations fail to adopt this philosophy baffles and troubles me.

Just Don't Do It

For more than a decade, sportswear giants Nike and Adidas-Solomon have faced intense international pressure to change the treatment of workers in Asian factories. Nike, the world's number one athletic shoe company, alone subcontracts eleven factories in Indonesia, which produce between 45 and 55 million pairs of shoes a year, most of which end up in the U.S. market. In response to public revelations of worker abuse, both rivals made concerted efforts to shed their sweatshop image.[13]

Perhaps like me, you considered the issue resolved and thought that the companies had moved to more enlightened employment practices globally. A 2002 report from Oxfam Community Aid Abroad indicates otherwise. The Australian nongovernmental group charges that neither Nike nor Adidas is doing nearly enough to curb the mistreatment of workers in its factories in Indonesia. Tens of thousands of workers allegedly live in extreme poverty and labor under dangerous conditions; they experience frequent injuries on cutting machines and inhale toxic fumes without protection. Workers who join trade unions fear losing their jobs or being attacked. "Factory managers abuse and harass us because they think it will increase our productivity," testifies one worker in the Oxfam report. "Humans cannot work like that. We are not machines."

Nike claims that it already knew of the abuses and is addressing them through its collaboration with the Global Alliance for Workers and Communities. But according to Oxfam, the Global Alliance is funded by Nike to run a program of assessment, training, and development in fewer than thirty of the more than nine hundred factories that make the company's products.

The fact that the two image-conscious clothes manufacturers, already under close international scrutiny and with tremendous capacity, can perform so poorly indicates either a lack of will or poor corporate oversight. The reason matters less than the results: "Both companies have refused to put in place structural reforms which would ensure decent wages and conditions," the Oxfam report concludes.

COOPERATIVE VALUES

"A law of indiscriminate profit is being globalized, and by its application all too many corporations contribute to the abuse of human rights in poor countries."[14] This declaration sounds as if it came straight off the podium of the antiglobalization protests that filled the streets of Genoa, Italy, on the occasion of the World Trade Organization (WTO) meeting in the summer of 2001. An Italian did in fact share this opinion with me, but surprisingly, he is Riccardo Bagni, the chief executive of Coop Italia, one of the biggest commercial enterprises in all of Europe.

Coop Italia, with headquarters in Bologna, is made up of a group of cooperatives operating in the banking, insurance, and retail sectors. The conglomerate operates around fifty superstores, a thousand supermarkets, and two hundred discount stores covering all of Italy. Its total sales turned the tills for close to $10 billion for 2001.

The cooperative movement was born in Italy more than a hundred years ago to stimulate fair market conditions for workers who did not have ready access to capital. Taking up this legacy, Coop Italia was launched in 1947 as an international buying office for the cooperatives that were still in business.

Phenomenal growth over the years has pushed the company into constant organizational change. But the original ethos of the enterprise stands firm. "Coop Italia is a company comprising people, not capital," Riccardo declares.

Coop Italia's standout efforts to improve labor practices around the globe give his claim credence. The company purchases food and nonfood products from nearly twenty-five hundred suppliers worldwide. In 2001, it bought nearly $50 million in goods from Asian countries alone; most of its textiles and rugs, for example, come from China, India, Pakistan, and Bangladesh.

The company began considering a code of conduct for its supplier network in the mid-1990s. Riccardo had been appointed vice chairman for the company's nonfood products with direct responsibility for private brand management and quality assurance. He made it a priority to set consistent labor standards wherever Coop Italia conducted business in the world. "I wanted to make sure that the respect of workers, especially for those belonging to the weaker ends of society, was a prime value at our company," he says.

Italians love soccer, so Riccardo could not think of a better venue than the World Football Championship in 1998 for introducing the concept of fair trade. Coop Italia heavily promoted and stocked on store shelves a soccer ball that it called the "Ethics Ball," made in Pakistan at a higher-than-normal production price to ensure a living wage. Coop Italia also made sure that no child labor was involved in the ball's production.

The Ethics Ball campaign never was intended to be a one-off marketing ploy. It gave Coop Italia a tangible symbol for expressing a much broader, systematic policy that would guide corporate purchasing going forward. In fact, at the time, Coop

Italia was in the process of being certified as a Social Accountability 8000 (SA8000) company.

The SA8000 is an international standard that certifies
through independent auditors that a company and its suppliers
are carrying out fair labor practices. Its architect is Social
Accountability International, a human rights organization based
in New York. The group was inspired by Levi Strauss's initiatives in the early 1990s to screen its entire supply chain for the
inhumane treatment of workers.[15] Social Accountability International discovered that other corporations shared Levi
Strauss's concerns but struggled to monitor all of their business
partners. On the other end of the production chain, suppliers
were finding it impractical to comply with distinct codes of conduct for each of its overseas customers. The SA8000 fills the
void for an accessible benchmark.

"The SA8000 provides our company with the tools we need
to select suppliers as well as monitor them," confirms Riccardo.
Coop Italia earned certification for its own store-brand food
products in December 1998. Soon after, the company established a system to oversee all of its international purchasing. It
works closely with second-party agencies to monitor and verify compliance. For suppliers found to be operating in violation
of its code of conduct, Coop Italia provides intensive training
on how they can adopt plans that will move them progressively
toward compliance.

One such incident arose with a fruit supplier in Africa. Del
Monte Kenya provides Coop-brand pineapples. Although the
corporate parent, Del Monte Foods Company, had signed off
on Coop Italia's code of conduct, independent auditors inspect-
ing its plantation in Kenya found major problems: violations
that related especially to safety conditions and the workers'

Core Values for a Global Economy

Coop Italia lives by the nine principles of Social Accountability 8000:

1. Child Labor—The company shall not employ children under 15 years of age.

2. Forced Labor—The company shall not employ anyone who is not free to suspend a work contract.

3. Health and Safety—The company must guarantee a secure and healthy working environment.

4. Freedom of Association—The company shall not prohibit, oppose or penalize union activity.

5. Discrimination—The company shall select employees on the basis of their competence and capabilities, offering them equal opportunities and conditions.

6. Disciplinary Practices—The company shall treat all workers with dignity and respect and prohibit use of unacceptable physical discipline.

7. Remuneration—The company shall assure its workers the economic conditions for a dignified standard of living.

8. Work Hours—The company shall not force workers to exceed a 40-hour work week, nor ask for more than 12 hours of overtime, nor ask employees habitually to work overtime.

9. Management—The company shall implement a system to monitor and verify that its suppliers are fulfilling this code of conduct, and provide corrective actions in the case of violations.

Source: Coop Italia corporate document, n.d.

right to form a union. Del Monte Kenya at first denied the audit report, then resisted making changes. Local human rights organizations and the Kenyan government backed the workers and turned up the heat on the fruit producer to make changes. Coop Italia helped facilitate negotiations among all the parties, and Del Monte Kenya made corrective actions.

Although many transnational corporations disdain trade unions and human rights groups in the markets where they operate, Coop Italia sees them as allies. Being local, they can alert the company to the most serious problems that exist at a manufacturing facility or agricultural plantation. "They are essential partners not only to inform us regarding possible abuses," asserts Riccardo, "but they also connect us to the people who can help to make things right."

The globalization of labor is a matter of fierce debate. As happens in many debates, the extremes grab the spotlight: unrestricted free contract versus sweatshop exploitation. Fortunately, a vanguard of corporations is showing how positive, long-term partnerships can be built with workers and the social sector to mutual advantage.

Conclusion

From Success to Significance

I wrote this book above all for people who work in corporations. So many of my friends and colleagues tell me they feel trapped. Although the corporation may offer them the best platform and set of rewards to develop their career, they wonder whether they are selling out—selling out their life priorities, selling out their integrity, selling out the promises they make to themselves and to other people.

Lots of us are too cynical to believe it can be otherwise. Isn't that simply the price you pay to join the corporation?

The dozens of case studies I feature in this book show that it can be otherwise. In fact, the evidence indicates that a business will thrive once it aligns the ethos of the company with the values that drive its customers and its own workers. To get there, the people inside a company need to ask themselves, again and again, one question: What are we in business for?

I keep coming back to the message that Russell Ackoff gave to his students at the Wharton School: "Profit is a means, not an end." That wisdom hit home for me most powerfully when I was CEO of a start-up company in the late 1990s. At the time, new technologies were forcing corporations to rethink the way they ran their business operations. The blur of innovation made it difficult for senior managers to separate the real from the hype. My company saw an opportunity amid that confusion; we aimed to become the trusted adviser matching real business needs with real working technology. I'll spare you the rest of the pitch.

Back then, I spared no words or effort on behalf of my company. Anyone who has passed through fire and storm to launch a business will ever forget the experience. I worked with my executive team eighty or ninety hours a week to write a business plan (and thereafter rewrite it daily, or so it seemed) and to develop financial projections, sales strategies, technology platforms, and operational protocols. All the while, we were out courting potential customers and investors, making the rounds to blue-chip venture capitalists and corporate fund managers looking for the best partners to fuel our enterprise.

After nine months and few victories, it looked as if our ship finally was coming in. We were introduced to Michael Milken, who was busy stitching together a group of companies under one canopy named Knowledge Universe (KU). Our company fit well into KU's strategic plan, and our services were quite complementary to some of the assets Michael already had acquired. Over a series of meetings with him and his chief advisers, we negotiated the details of our business relationship. Michael wanted KU to be the sole investor in our company, and he pledged tens of millions of dollars of financing as long as we met a schedule of performance benchmarks. In exchange, KU would acquire a huge slice of our company.

Although Michael's legacy will be forever linked to junk bonds, corporate raiders, and a prison sentence, he dealt with our team in complete good faith and earned my respect. He is a tough-as-nails negotiator, mind you, and possesses the most brilliant financial mind I have ever encountered.

As we were closing in on a deal with KU, I decided to jump off the spinning carousel to clear my head. I took my family to Lake Tahoe for a few days of hiking and boating. Midway through the holiday, Michael gave me a call. We went over a few final details to our mutual satisfaction, and then he put to me his final test: "David, I trust you realize that once we make this deal, this company will be your life."

I swallowed hard, told him I completely understood, and the call ended with the exchange of a few pleasantries. In fact, his words thudded on top of me like a ton of bricks. The impact was immediate and served as a catalyst for a kind of spiritual awakening.

It was not as if I was doing anything that violated my moral compass. I can imagine any number of people who, being in the same position, could accept the investment, and it would be the best possible decision for them to make. But I was forced to confront my motivation, that is, my purpose for being in this business. Down deep I knew the reason: I was hawking widgets, pieces of technology. I had no passion, none at all, to help corporations solve their operational dilemmas and become more efficient. To be completely honest, I was in it for the money.

This will be your life. Once off the telephone and returning to my family in the cabin, I put together a mental inventory of the things that I deeply valued. I saw four small children who had not seen much of their dad for the previous year. I thought of my love for teaching at the university, my passion for writing, and the profound meaning I gained promoting human development in poverty-stricken countries. What was the price tag I could put on all that? *Priceless,* my inner voice replied.

I returned home several days later with the clarity I went looking for. I would resign. Most difficult of all was sharing the decision with my executive team, with whom I had labored and made considerable financial sacrifice. Meeting with them was the second test of my conviction, because I knew they would try to talk me out of it. I certainly don't blame them for trying. We were finally on the cusp of receiving our reward. My pulling out of the company meant disaster. Michael was investing in our management team, a remarkably talented group of professionals, as much as our business. Although I felt terrible for letting them down, I knew that I could not go forward. We floated the option of accepting KU's investment and then six to twelve months down the road finding a new CEO. But I rejected that idea out of hand. I was sure of Michael's intention, and playing that game would be nothing short of betrayal.

The next day, I contacted Michael and explained my decision to step down as CEO. He was surprised at first, but our conversation soon turned philosophical. He shared that he too believed in using one's talents to make a meaningful contribution to the world and made note of his own impressive philanthropic work. Creating financial wealth enabled him to do those things, he added, implying I was making a false choice between significance and financial success.

What I said in reply to Michael—and believe firmly to this day—is that living with soul transcends the matter of money. One cannot give enough money away to heal a broken spirit. Nor, for that matter, does turning one's back on money ensure the slightest degree of enlightenment. The person who lives his or her life in pursuit of success—be that measured by wealth, fame, or social status—will be sorely disenchanted with the pot at the end of the rainbow. Success alone cannot satisfy our deepest longings for significance.

Each individual holds within a passion for significance that awaits discovery. The actual makeup of that dream is not the same for each person and is a blend of innate skills and personality, social circumstance, and lived experience. Figuring out the origin of the dream is wasted speculation. Realizing our passion and pursuing it is our life's work. When we follow that path, we are never disappointed by the results, whatever they may turn out to be.

I was never a big fan of the television series *Ally McBeal*, to be honest, but I must admit that I was touched by the final episode. Ally told her colleagues that she was moving to New York from Boston after five years with her firm (exactly the duration of the series). "You're the soul of this place," sighed one of her colleagues lamenting her departure. "In some way, you've become the soul of all of us."

At this moment, the corporation sorely needs leaders—not people with titles, but true leaders at every level of the corporate ladder—to live with soul. In my case, I had to leave the helm of a company to pursue my path toward significance. That may be the risk other corporate workers may have to take as well. I am inclined to believe, however, that for most people, it is not a new path but a truth about themselves that awaits discovery. Once they start living out of that discovery, they inspire everyone who surrounds them.

No greater tribute could we receive from a coworker: *You, my friend, are the soul of this place.*

Notes

INTRODUCTION

1. R. Howard, "Values Make the Company: An Interview with Robert Haas," *Harvard Business Review,* Sept.-Oct. 1990, p. 134.

2. As told to C. Hymowitz, "Managers Must Respond to Employee Concerns About Honest Business," *Wall Street Journal,* Feb. 19, 2002, p. B1.

3. Walker Information, *Commitment in the Workplace: The 1999 National Employee Benchmark Study* (Indianapolis: Walker Information and Hudson Institute, 1999). Walker conducted the same survey in 2001; the results show that employee loyalty did not change notably in two years: Walker Information, *Commitment in the Workplace: The 2001 National Employee Benchmark Study* (Indianapolis: Walker Information, 2001).

4. W. H. Whyte, *The Organization Man* (New York: Doubleday, 1956), p. 12.

5. Based on interview with Tom Higa, Nov. 2002; B. Snider, "Chevron's Big Spill in Haight: Bad Will," *San Francisco Examiner,* Apr. 23, 1989, pp. A1, A19; "Chevron Station May Stay Open in the Haight," *San Francisco Chronicle,* Apr. 27, 1989, p. A5; V. Kershner, "Popular Haight Gas Station to Stay Open," *San Francisco Chronicle,* May 13, 1989, p. A3; M. Zane, "New Law to Save Gas Stations," *San Francisco Chronicle,* July 23, 1991, p. A17.

6. Snider, "Big Spill."

7. Interview, Tom Higa.

8. Snider, "Big Spill."

9. Based on interview with former San Francisco mayor Art Agnos (1988–1992), Apr. 2002.

10. J. Schmidt, *Stakeholder Perspectives: A Key to Success in the New Economy* (Chicago: Towers Perrin, 2000).

11. J. L. Seglin, "How Business Can Be Good (and Why Being Good Is Good for Business)," *Sojourners*, Jan.-Feb. 2000, pp. 17–18.

12. Cone/Roper, *Cause-Related Trends Report: Evolution of Cause Branding* (Boston: Cone, 1999).

13. Hill & Knowlton, *2001 Corporate Citizen Watch* (New York: Hill & Knowlton, 2001).

14. Hill & Knowlton, 2001.

15. Washington Post/ABCNews Poll analysis in G. Langer, "Confidence in Business: Was Low and Still Is," *ABCNews.com*, July 1, 2002.

16. J. Bandler and J. Hechinger, "SEC Says Xerox Misled Investors," *Wall Street Journal*, Apr. 12, 2002. C. H. Deutsch, "Xerox Revises Revenue Data, Tripling Error First Reported," *New York Times*, June 29, 2002.

17. J. Frooman, "Socially Irresponsible and Illegal Behavior and Shareholder Wealth," *Business and Society*, 1997, *36*, 221–249.

18. G. Winter, "Timber Company Reduces Cutting of Old-Growth Trees," *New York Times*, Mar. 27, 2002, p. A14.

19. Winter, "Timber Company Reduces Cutting of Old-Growth Trees."

CHAPTER ONE

1. "Declining Levels of Employee Trust Are a Major Threat to Corporate Competitiveness, Watson Wyatt Study Finds," Watson Wyatt press release, July 25, 2002.

2. The background material for Clif Bar and all quotations in this section are drawn from an interview with G. Erickson, July 2002.

3. J. Christoffersen, "Long Admired, GE Adjusts to New Environment," Associated Press, Mar. 23, 2002.

4. J. Sonnenfeld, "Expanding Without Managing," *New York Times*, June 12, 2002.

5. The background material for CalEnergy/MidAmerican and all quotations are drawn from an interview with D. Sokol, July 2002.

6. C. Collins, "Let's Close the CEO Salary Loophole," *Dollars and Sense*, July-Aug. 1997, p. 4. J. A. Byrne, "How to Fix Corporate Governance," *BusinessWeek*, May 6, 2002, p. 72.

7. P. Krugman, "Enemies of Reform," *New York Times*, May 21, 2002.

8. "Corporate Leaders Gain Even as Their Firms Go Bankrupt," *Financial Times*, July 31, 2002.

9. C. Berthelsen, "E-Trade Ekes Out Slim Profit," *San Francisco Chronicle*, July 18, 2002.

10. R. Hemsley, "Losing My Stake in the Economy," *New York Times*, July 20, 2002, p. A25.

11. R. Shiller, "Celebrity CEOs Share the Blame for Street Scandals," *Wall Street Journal*, June 27, 2002, p. A20.

12. P. H. O'Neill, "Rebuilding Trust in Corporate America," remarks to the U.S. Chamber of Commerce, Washington, D.C., July 10, 2002.

13. D. Leonhardt, "Tell the Good News, Then Cash In," *New York Times*, Apr. 7, 2002.

14. D. Leonhardt, "Slivers of Support for Shackling Corporate Pay," *New York Times*, July 13, 2002.

15. Research from Frederic W. Cook and Company, an executive compensation consulting firm based in New York, cited in Leonhardt, "Shackling Corporate Pay," 2002.

16. P. Krugman, "America's Poor Standards," *New York Times*, May 17, 2002.

17. D. Leonhardt, "Stock Options Said to Be Not as Widespread as Backers Say," *New York Times*, July 18, 2002.

18. K. Pender, "Is Coke's Big Move Real Thing?" *San Francisco Chronicle*, July 16, 2002.

19. W. Buffet, "Chairman's Letter," Berkshire Hathaway, 2001.

20. Byrne, 2002.

21. D. Leonhardt, "Qwest Officials Made Millions in Stock Sales," *New York Times*, July 30, 2002. S. Young, "Qwest to Restate $950 Million of Revenue Tied to 'Swap' Deals," *Wall Street Journal*, Sept. 23, 2002.

22. Teddy Roosevelt as quoted by U.S. Senator J. McCain, address to the National Press Club, July 11, 2002.

23. K. Talaski, "Sweetheart Exec Deals Cost Kmart Millions," *Detroit News*, May 17, 2002.

24. "Executive Suite Scandals," *San Francisco Chronicle*, June 14, 2002. A. R. Sorkin, "Founder of Adelphia and Two Sons Arrested," *New York Times*, July 25, 2002.

25. J. S. Lublin, "Loans to Corporate Officers Unlikely to Cease Soon," *Wall Street Journal*, July 10, 2002.

26. "U.S. CEO Compensation Survey," Mercer Human Resource Consulting, May 2002. D. Gilbertson, "Top Executives Use Firm as Lender of First Resort," *Arizona Republic*, May 28, 2002.

27. R. Simon, "Senate Votes to Ban Company Loans to Top Executives," *Los Angeles Times*, July 13, 2002.

28. W. C. Powers and others, "Special Investigation by the Investigative Committee of the Board of Directors of Enron Corp.," Feb. 2, 2002.

29. D. Kadlec, "Corporate Greed: Eight Remedies," *Time*, June 17, 2002.

30. C. Hymowitz, "Building a Board That's Independent, Strong, and Effective," *Wall Street Journal*, Nov. 19, 2002.

31. Hymowitz, 2002, p. B1.

32. J. Lublin, "Splitting Posts of Chairman, CEO Catches On," *Wall Street Journal*, Nov. 11, 2002, pp. B1, B3.

33. Lublin, 2002, p. B3.

34. Kadlec, 2002.

35. L. Lavelle, "How Shareholder Votes Are Legally Rigged," *BusinessWeek*, May 20, 2002.

36. W. B. Hewlett quoted in S. Lohr, "Corporate Boards Are Supposed to Represent Shareholders. Why Aren't They More Democratic?" *New York Times*, May 6, 2002, p. C4.

37. B. Franklin, *Poor Richard's Almanack* (Mount Vernon, N.Y.: Peter Pauper Press, 1983), p. 22.

38. The background material on Franklin Resources and all quotations in this section are drawn from an interview with C. B. Johnson, May 2002.

39. C. B. Johnson, "Letter to Shareholders," *Franklin Resources Annual Report 2001*.

CHAPTER TWO

1. P. J. Howe, "Merrill Agrees to $100m Settlement," *Boston Globe*, May 22, 2002. "Merrill Lynch's Deal," *New York Times*, May 22, 2002.

2. G. Morgenson, "Lawsuit Says Salomon Gave Special Deals to Rich Clients," *New York Times*, July 18, 2002. "Those Ugly Insider IPOs," *Wall Street Journal*, Aug. 29, 2002. G. Morgenson, "Salomon Memo Hints at Favor on New Stock Issues," *New York Times*, Aug. 29, 2002.

3. D. Feldstein, "Special-Purpose Vehicles Used to Control Market, Credit Rating," *Houston Chronicle*, Jan. 28, 2002.

4. The framework for J. Alexander's experience at Enron draws heavily from J. Schwartz, "An Enron Unit Chief Warned, and Was Rebuffed," *New York Times*, Feb. 20, 2002. Alexander confirmed the accuracy of Schwartz's article and provided additional commentary in an interview conducted in Mar. 2002.

5. The background material on Spinnaker Exploration and all quotations in this section are drawn from an interview with J. Alexander and an interview with R. Jarvis, May 2002.

6. The background material for Wild Planet Toys and all quotations

in this section are drawn from an interview with D. Grossman, Apr. 2002.

7. D. Foust and D. Henry, "Has Coke Been Playing Accounting Games?" *BusinessWeek*, May 13, 2002. B. Martinez, "Merck Booked $12.4 Billion It Never Collected," *Wall Street Journal*, July 8, 2002. Bandler and Maremont, 2002.

8. K. Eichenwald, "Waste Management Executives Are Named in SEC Accusation," *New York Times*, Mar. 27, 2002.

9. P. O'Neil as quoted in D. Wessel, "Why the Bad Guys of the Boardroom Emerged en Masse," *Wall Street Journal*, June 20, 2002.

10. Interview with D. Tarantino, May 2002.

11. E. Church, "Audits Often Secondary to Consulting: Survey," *Globe and Mail* (Toronto), Apr. 22, 2002.

12. Interview with Tarantino.

13. Interview with A. Brief, Apr. 2002.

14. Reverend Doctor D. Littlefair, eulogy delivered at the funeral of Arthur Andersen on Jan. 13, 1947, as quoted in *Harper's Magazine*, June 2002.

15. The background material for Southwest Airlines and all quotations in this section drawn from an interview with B. Montgomery, Apr. 2002.

CHAPTER THREE

1. The background is drawn from J. L. Kwan and T. Walker, " 'Big Box' Measures Not Just About Size," *San Jose Mercury News*, Feb. 28, 2002.

2. Forum with M. Krasney, KQED, Feb. 26, 2002. See also W. Anderson, "Opinion: Free Materials Can't Build Social Responsibility," *Campbell Reporter*, Oct. 10, 2001.

3. "Vote No on N in Mountain View," *San Jose Mercury News*, Feb. 25, 2002. "Vote No on C," *San Jose Mercury News*, Feb. 25, 2002.

4. T. Walker, "Ikea's Win Stands Final Tally Shows," *San Jose Mercury News*, Mar. 14, 2002. A. Pence, "Ikea Victory in East Palo Alto," *San Francisco Chronicle*, Mar. 6, 2002.

5. B. W. Carlson, "A Corporate Bermuda Triangle," *Christian Science Monitor*, May 21, 2002.

6. D. C. Johnston, "Vote on an Offshore Tax Plan Is Testing Company's Values," *New York Times*, May 9, 2002. D. C. Johnston, "Tax Treaties with Small Nations Turn into a New Shield for Profits," *New York Times*, Apr. 16, 2002.

7. As reported in Carlson, 2002.

8. "The Bermuda Tax Triangle," *New York Times*, May 13, 2002. For

other examples of public outrage, see A. Sloan, "The Tax-Free Bermuda Getaway," *Newsweek*, Apr. 15, 2002. D. R. Francis, "Tax Revenues Vanish as Firms Move from U.S. to Bermuda," *Christian Science Monitor*, May 22, 2002.

9. S. Sleigh as quoted in Johnston, May 9, 2002.

10. P. Plitch and G. R. Simpson, "Bowing to Pressure, Stanley Works Drops Plans for Bermuda Tax Move," *Wall Street Journal*, Aug. 2, 2002.

11. Cone, *Cause-Related Trends Report* (Boston: Cone, 1999).

12. S. Adkins, *Cause-Related Marketing: Who Cares Wins* (New York: Butterworth-Heineman, 1999).

13. Hill & Knowlton, 2001.

14. The background material for Ahold is drawn from an interview with N. Gale, director of public relations at Ahold, Oct. 2002. See also J. Nelson and S. Zadek, *Partnership Alchemy: New Social Partnerships in Europe* (Copenhagen: Copenhagen Center, 2000).

15. The background material for Timberland and the J. Swartz quotations are drawn from Timberland corporate documents and an interview with R. Matchett, director of corporate relations at Timberland, July 2002.

16. The background material on Sexual Assault Support Services and quotations in this section are drawn from an interview with M. Franzosa, Aug. 2002.

17. Council on Foundations, *Measuring the Value of Corporate Citizenship* (Washington, D.C.: Council on Foundations, 1996).

18. The background material on e-GM and quotations in this section are drawn from an interview with C. MacNeil, May 2002.

19. Interview with M. Hogan, June 2002.

20. As cited in e-GM corporate documents. See also A. Dietderich, "GM Sees Charity in Patents," *Crain's Detroit Business*, Nov. 12, 2001.

21. The background material on Hanna Anderrson and all quotations in this section are drawn from an interview with G. Denhart and her staff, May 2002.

22. Interview with J. Ritchie, June 2002.

23. Interview with J. Mills, May 2002.

24. Center for Corporate Community Relations, *Making the Business Case: Determining the Value of Corporate Community Involvement* (Chestnut Hill, Mass.: Boston College, 2000).

CHAPTER FOUR

1. T. Wallack, "Cell Phone Giant Called 'Unfair to Consumers,'" *San Francisco Chronicle*, July 3, 2002.

2. Background material on Ven-A-Care and all quotations in this section are drawn from an interview with Z. Bentley, July 2002.

3. For more background, see J. Appleby, "Feds Probe Drug Pricing," *USA Today*, Apr. 6, 2000. D. Cauchon, "Americans Pay More for Medicine," *USA Today*, Nov. 10, 1999. J. Appleby, "Drugmakers Accused of Price Scheme," *USA Today*, Sept. 27, 2002.

4. J. Appleby, "Drugmakers Accused of 'Unethical' Pricing," *USA Today*, Sept. 27, 2000.

5. "Report: Bayer to Pay $14 Million in Probe of Drug Prices," Associated Press, Sept. 18, 2002.

6. F. Thompson, "Should Pharmaceutical Companies Be Able to Advertise Directly to Patients?" *Pharmaceutical Journal*, July 14, 2001, pp. 45–46.

7. J. Judd, "Truth in Advertising? FDA Says Many Prescription Drug Ads Are Deceptive," *ABCNews.com*, Jan. 3, 2001. C. Adams and A. Grimes, "FDA Says Some Drug-Ad Images May Be Misleading to Consumers," *Wall Street Journal*, May 4, 2001.

8. C. Adams, "Looser Lips for Food and Drug Companies?" *Wall Street Journal*, Sept. 17, 2002. V. O'Connell, "Ad Firms to the Rescue—of Drug Makers," *Wall Street Journal*, Apr. 19, 2002.

9. S. Boseley, "Scandal of Scientists Who Take Money for Papers Ghostwritten by Drug Companies," *Guardian* (U.K.), Feb. 7, 2002. M. Petersen, "Madison Ave. Plays Growing Role in the Business of Drug Research," *New York Times*, Nov. 22, 2002.

10. The entire issue of the journal evaluates biomedical research process: *Journal of the American Medical Association*. June 5, 2002.

11. M. Petersen, "Suit Says Company Promoted Drug in Exam Rooms," *New York Times*, May 15, 2002. L. Kowalczyk, "Drug Company Push on Doctors Disclosed," *Boston Globe*, May 19, 2002. M. W. Walsh, "When a Buyer for Hospitals Has a Stake in Drugs It Buys," *New York Times*, Mar. 26, 2002.

12. E. Sanders, "Banks Say They Release Customers' Data," *Los Angeles Times*, June 10, 1999.

13. Background material on the ServiceMaster Company and all quotations in this section are drawn from an interview with B. Pollard, Oct. 2002. Background material also comes from C. W. Pollard, *The Soul of the Firm* (Grand Rapids, Mich.: Zondervan: 2000).

14. J. L. Heskett and others, "Putting the Service-Profit Chain to Work," *Harvard Business Review*, Mar.–Apr. 1994, pp. 164–174.

15. Background material on Odwalla and all quotations in this section are drawn from an interview with G. Steltenpohl, Mar. 2002. Also

helpful was an interview with W. Rosenzweig, former Odwalla executive and founder of the Republic of Tea, Mar. 2002.

CHAPTER FIVE

1. As quoted in Pollard, 2000, p. 1.

2. S. Greenhouse, "Suits Say Wal-Mart Forces Workers to Toil off the Clock," *New York Times*, June 25, 2002. See also B. Ehrenreich, "Two-Tiered Morality," *New York Times*, June 30, 2002.

3. M. Orey, "Lawsuits Abound from Workers Seeking Overtime Pay," *Wall Street Journal*, May 30, 2002.

4. Greenhouse, 2002.

5. Greenhouse, 2002.

6. Greenhouse, 2002.

7. U.S. Department of Health and Human Services, "The 2002 HHS Poverty Guidelines," *Federal Register*, Feb. 14, 2002, pp. 6931–6933.

8. S. Zuckerman, "How Providian Misled Cardholders," *San Francisco Chronicle*, May 5, 2002.

9. C. Berthelsen, "Providian to Lay Off 1,300," *San Francisco Chronicle*, Aug. 4, 2002.

10. M. Musgrove, "Intel to Cut 4,000 Jobs as Earnings Fall Short," *Washington Post*, July 17, 2002.

11. A. Downs, *Corporate Executions* (New York: American Management Association, 1995). A. Downs, "The Wages of Downsizing," *Mother Jones*, July–Aug. 1996, pp. 26–31.

12. Background material on Malden Mills and all quotations in this section are drawn from an interview with A. Feuerstein in Aug. 2002.

13. Background material on Boeing and U.S. West and all quotations in this section are drawn from an interview with C. Fred, Apr. 2002.

14. Background material on United Airlines and all quotations in this section are drawn from an interview with G. Stockton, June 2000. See also K. Kiser, "E-Learning Takes Off at United Airlines," *Training Magazine*, 1999, *36*, pp. 66–70.

15. R. Beyster, founder and CEO of Science Applications International Corp., as quoted in M. Kelly, "The Truth About Stock Options," *Business Ethics*, 2000, *14*, 4.

16. J. Logue and M. Kelly, "It's Time to Renew Our National Enthusiasm for Employee Ownership," *Business Ethics*, 2000, *14*, pp. 16–17.

17. J. Yates and M. Kelly, "The 100 Largest Majority-Owned Companies (and What Makes Them Great)," *Business Ethics*, 2000, *14*, 10–15.

18. Yates and Kelly, 2000.

19. According to a study by Westward Pay Strategies, as cited in M. Kelly, "The Truth About Stock Options," *Business Ethics*, 2000, *14*, p. 4.

20. Background information on Chatsworth Products and all quotations in this section are drawn from an interview with J. Cabral, July 2002.

CHAPTER SIX

1. Background material for Monsanto in Anniston is drawn from M. Grunwald, "Monsanto Held Liable for PCB Dumping," *Washington Post*, Feb. 23, 2002. D. Teather, "Monsanto Found Guilty of Polluting," *Guardian* (U.K.), Feb. 25, 2002. D. Firestone, "Alabama Jury Says Monsanto Polluted Town," *New York Times*, Feb. 23, 2002.

2. Background material on Pura Vida Coffee and all quotations are drawn from an interview with J. Sage, July 2002. In the interest of full disclosure, Pura Vida also markets a line of coffee called SojoBlend to benefit *Sojourners* magazine, of which I am executive editor.

3. Background material on MacMillan Bloedel and all quotations in this section are drawn from an interview with L. Coady, June 2002.

4. Background material on Danone and Stonyfield Farm, as well as all quotations in this section, are drawn from an interview with G. Hirshberg and his senior staff, May 2002.

5. J. Rose, "Selling His Soul to Dannon?" *Fortune Small Business*, Dec. 3, 2002.

6. S. Schmidheiny, R. Chase, and L. DeSimone, *Signals of Change* (Geneva: World Council for Sustainable Development, 1997).

7. S. Hart and G. Ahuja, "Does It Pay to Be Green? An Empirical Examination of the Relationship Between Emission Reduction and Firm Performance," *Business Strategy and the Environment*, 1996, *5*, 30–37.

8. A. Kirby, "Brent Spar's Long Saga," *BBCNews Online*, Nov. 25, 1998. "Protests Mount Against Shell Oil-Rig," *San Francisco Examiner News Service*, June 18, 1995.

9. J. Boulden, "Q and A with John Elkington, President of Sustain-Ability," *CNNfn*, Sept. 30, 2000.

10. M. Regester, "The Role of Corporate Social Responsibility in Managing Reputation," *Ethical Corporation*, Feb. 2002, pp. 21–22.

11. Background material on Shell and all quotations in this section are drawn from an interview with A. Burke, July 2002.

12. R. M. Stapleton, *Protecting the Source: Land Conservation and the Future of America's Drinking Water* (San Francisco: Trust for Public Land, 1997). World Resources Institute, "Valuing Eco-System

Services," in *World Resources 1998–99* (Washington, D.C.: World Resources Institute, 1998).

CHAPTER SEVEN

1. Background material for B. Campbell and the class action suit against Cracker Barrel is drawn from L. Bivins, "More Plaintiffs Added to Discrimination Suit Against Cracker Barrel," Gannett News Service, Apr. 11, 2002. "NAACP Joins Race Discrimination Class Action Lawsuit Against Cracker Barrel Restaurant Chain," NAACP press release, Apr. 11, 2002.

2. Bivins, 2002.

3. "Cracker Barrel Faces a Civil Rights Lawsuit," *Decatur Daily*, Dec. 14, 2001.

4. J. Adamson, *The Denny's Story: How a Company in Crisis Resurrected Its Good Name* (New York: Wiley, 2000).

5. R. Mokhiber, "The Ten Worst Corporations of 1994," *Multinational Monitor*, Dec. 1994, pp. 9–18. See also H. Kohn, "Service with a Sneer," *New York Times Magazine*, Nov. 6, 1994, pp. 42–47. S. Wollenberg, "Minorities Make Their Mark in New Denny's Commercial," Associated Press, Jan. 14, 1997.

6. K. Hohman, "Chatting with Jim Adamson: Denny's CEO Discusses Battling Back from a Racist Corporate Culture," *About.com*, Mar. 21, 2002.

7. Adamson, 2000. Hohman, 2002.

8. K. Jacobs, "Suits Shine Light on Workplace Diversity," Reuters, February 10, 2002.

9. "Best Companies for Minorities," *Fortune*, July 8, 2002. Advantica finished number three on the list in 2002.

10. Quoted in Hohman, 2002.

11. A. W. Blumrosen and R. G. Blumrosen, *The Realities of Intentional Job Discrimination in Metropolitan America* (Newark, N.J.: Rutgers Law School, 2002).

12. Blumrosen and Blumrosen, 2002, p. 1.

13. Background material for Charles Schwab Company and all quotations in this section are drawn from an interview with P. Jackson, Apr. 2002.

14. "Diversity in the New Millennium," *Working Woman*, Mar. 2000, p. 66.

15. Background material is drawn from Xerox corporate documents and an interview with Donna Lipari, a senior director in corporate public relations at Xerox, Aug. 2002.

16. Letter from P. C. McColough, Xerox corporate documents, May 1968. Xerox chairman J. C. Wilson also signed the letter.

17. Interview with E. Hicks, Aug. 2002.

18. Background material on the Hispanic Association for Professional Advancement and all quotations in this section are drawn from an interview with A. Fernández-Campfield, Aug. 2002.

19. Interview with Hicks, 2002.

20. R. A. Friedman and C. Deinard, *Black Caucus Groups at Xerox Corp.* (Boston: Harvard Business School Case Study, 1991).

21. Background material on B&Q in this section is drawn from "B&Q's Employment Policy for the over 50s." [www.diy.co.uk]. Nov. 1, 2002.

22. Regester, 2002.

23. K. K. Spors, "Seeking a Spotlight on Minority Borrowers," *Wall Street Journal*, July 18, 2002. K. M. Kristof, "Fed Moves to Curb Predatory Lending," *Los Angeles Times*, Dec. 13, 2001. K. Platoni, "Big Setback for Predatory Lenders," *East Bay Express*, Oct. 3, 2001.

24. P. Beckett, "Citigroup May Pay $200 Million in FTC 'Predatory Lending' Case," *Wall Street Journal*, Sept. 6, 2002. P. Beckett and J. Hallinan, "Household May Pay $500 Million over 'Predatory' Loan Practices," *Wall Street Journal*, Oct. 11, 2002.

25. Study conducted by the Association of Community Organizations for Reform Now (ACORN), as cited in Platoni, 2001.

26. "Texas Life Insurers Surveyed on Race-Based Pricing," *Dallas Morning Journal*, Sept. 5, 2001. "MetLife Is Settling Bias Lawsuit," *New York Times*, Aug. 30, 2002. "Settlement Near for Insurer Accused of Overcharging Blacks," *New York Times*, Jan. 10, 2002.

27. Background material for Safeco is drawn from corporate documents and an interview with R. Lincoln, Safeco's director of community relations, June 2002.

28. Interview with D. Bird, Aug. 2002.

29. Interview with Bird, 2002.

30. Interview with Lincoln, 2002.

31. Interview with M. Wong, Aug. 2002.

32. Interview with M. M. Cerrudo, Aug. 2002.

33. The background material is drawn from SBC corporate documents.

34. L. Eurick, "Factors That Influence Minority Choice of a Long-Distance Service Provider" (paper presented to the National Congress for Community Economic Development Telecommunications Conference, Nov. 1997).

35. The background material on Telamon and all quotations in this section are drawn from an interview with A. Chen, Aug. 2002. See also,

"SBC Supplier Diversity Program Success Stories: Telamon Corporation," internal SBC document, 2002.

36. "Management Training Alliance," SBC corporate document, 2002.

CHAPTER EIGHT

1. The background material for K. Saro-Wiwa and Shell Oil Corporation is drawn from several sources: I. Okonta and O. Douglas, *Where Vultures Feast: Shell, Human Rights, and Oil in the Niger* (San Francisco: Sierra Club Books, 2001). "Remember Shell, Boycott Shell," *Multinational Monitor*, 1997, *18*, 4. C. Simpson, "Shell Overtures to Ogoni," *BBC News Online*, July 25, 2001. C. Ake, "Shelling Nigeria Ablaze," *Tell*, Jan. 29, 1996, pp. 34–35.

2. Background material for Placer Dome's experience with the Las Cristinas mine is drawn from three sources: M. Warner, "Placer Dome: Building Corporate Reputation and Trust in Venezuela," *Ethical Corporation*, Jan. 2002, pp. 12–15. *Case Study: Las Cristinas Gold Mine* (London: Natural Resources Cluster/Business Partners for Development, 2002). "Placer Dome Mine Falls Victim to Gold Slide," *Financial Times*, July 19, 1999.

3. All quotations in this section are drawn from an interview with K. Ferguson, Sept. 2002.

4. Background material for GrameenPhone and all quotations in this section are drawn from an interview with I. Qadir, Sept. 2002.

5. *Transparency International Bribe Payers Index 2002* (Berlin, Germany: Transparency International, 2002).

6. "West Creates Conditions for Corruption," *BBC News Online*, Mar. 25, 2002. L. McGregor, "Angola's Missing Billions," *Guardian* (U.K.), May 30, 2002. Global Witness, *All the President's Men: The Devastating Story of Oil and Banking in Angola's Privatised War* (London: Global Witness, 2002).

7. Global Witness, *A Crude Awakening: The Devastating Story of Oil and Banking in Angola's Privatised War* (London: Global Witness, 1999). *All the President's Men*, 2002.

8. Global Witness, *All the President's Men*, 2002.

9. "BP's Angolan Oil Interest," *BBC News Online*, Feb. 13, 2001.

10. The background material for BP and all quotations in this section are drawn from an interview with J. Browne and his senior staff, May 2002.

11. McGregor, 2002. T. Macalister, " 'Ethical' BP Linked to Angolan Claim: UK Group Targeted by State Oil Company in Corruption Allegations," *Guardian* (U.K.), Feb. 27, 2002.

12. Global Witness, *All the President's Men*, 2002, p. 6.

13. The background material in this section is drawn from *We Are Not Machines: Nike and Adidas Workers in Indonesia* (Melbourne, Australia: Oxfam Community Aid Abroad, 2002).

14. The background material on Coop Italia and all quotations in this section are drawn from an interview with R. Bagni, Sept. 2002.

15. The background material on Social Accountability International is drawn from an interview with D. Raines, communications director at Social Accountability International, Sept. 2002.

Acknowledgments

My two youngest sons, Jesse and Caelin, ask me every other day, "Daddy, are you done with that book yet? I really miss playing with you." The toll a writing project takes on a family deserves grateful recognition, not to mention lament for time lost. To my little ones, their siblings, Jade and Zak, and my remarkable wife, Wendy, I dedicate this book.

I acknowledge that this book may never have been written if it were not for my good friend and literary agent, Mark Tauber. Mark combed through the diverse range of articles I had written for the popular press over the past five years and pulled out a feature article I had written for *Sojourners* magazine titled "Saving the Corporate Soul." The Enron scandal—and the torrent of corporate corruption cases that followed once the dike broke open—was still months in the future. But Mark looked me straight in the eye: "This is the book you have to write." I listened. His partnership in this project did not end there; he has walked with me every step of the way.

My colleagues at *Sojourners* magazine and the University of San Francisco (USF) have carried heavier loads so that I could complete this work. They do so not only because they can, but also because they deeply believe in the message of this book and want it to get out to a mass audience. Jim Wallis and Jim Rice at *Sojourners* merit special mention. They inspire me to speak out publicly with wisdom and candor about things that matter. Lois Lorentzen and Mike Duffy at USF are remarkable companions as well, who effuse intellectual energy and passion for social justice into just about everything they do. Finally, I single out two of my business partners, Mark Boyce and Ron Posner, for practicing their craft with dignity and pride.

It's a wonderful feeling for an author to know he is with the right publisher. Lots of book companies made promises, but only one, Jossey-Bass, told me it absolutely had to publish this book because the material went to the core of what it sought to be. To prove the point, editor Susan Williams took the time to write a self-evaluation of Jossey-Bass based on my eight principles. After that, how could I choose another publisher? As a team, Susan, Julianna Gustafson, Todd Berman, and Erik Thrasher are beyond compare.

Profound thanks go to Rusty Springer (my guru), Don and Ruth Batstone (for being the kind of parents every child deserves), and Shannon McMillen Evans (logistical support and laughter). Most of this book was written in coffee shops in the Half Moon Bay area. Many thanks for the office space and friendly patience from my friends at the Half Moon Bay Coffee Company (especially Lisa, Sonny, Ken, and Joanna), Moonside Bakery, and Starbucks (Pacifica).

Gotta run. Two boys are waiting for me on the trampoline.

January 2003
Montara, California

DAVID BATSTONE

The Author

It is a rare set of skills that enables **David Batstone** to be active as a business entrepreneur, professor, and journalist. He was a founding editor of *Business 2.0* magazine and has been a contributor to the *New York Times*, *Wired*, the *Chicago Tribune*, *Spin*, and the *San Francisco Chronicle*. He is the recipient of two national journalist awards and was named the National Endowment for the Humanities Chair at the University of San Francisco for his work in technology and ethics. Batstone is also the executive editor of *Sojourners* magazine, the leading voice at the crossroads of politics, business, spirituality, and culture. Gifted as an entrepreneur, Batstone plays an executive role in a niche investment bank operating internationally in the entertainment and technology industries. During the 1980s, he founded and directed a nongovernmental agency dedicated to economic development and human rights in Latin America.

Index